CAIRO PAPERS IN SOCIAL SCIENCE
VOLUME 35   NUMBER 3

Understanding the Public Sector in Egyptian Cinema
A State Venture

Tamara C. Maatouk

THE AMERICAN UNIVERSITY IN CAIRO PRESS
CAIRO   NEW YORK

Cover photo: Miramar (1969) film poster. Artwork by Mohamad Abdulaziz, with reproduction assistance from Wahib Fahmy. Poster was commissioned by the General Egyptian Institution for
the Cinema and printed at Al-Nasr Press. Artwork was digitally restored by City Lights Posters. Courtesy of City Light Posters.

This paperback edition first published in 2023 by
The American University in Cairo Press
113 Sharia Kasr el Aini, Cairo, Egypt
420 Lexington Avenue, Suite 1644, New York, NY 10170
www.aucpress.com

First published in an electronic edition in 2019

Copyright © 2019, 2023 by the American University in Cairo Press

All rights reserved. No part of this publication may be reproduced, stored in a retrieval system, or transmitted in any form or by any means, electronic, mechanical, photocopying, recording, or otherwise, without the prior written permission of the publisher.

ISBN 978 1 649 03228 7

Library of Congress Cataloging-in-Publication Data applied for

1 2 3 4 5   27 26 25 24

Designed by Adam el-Sehemy

Contents

Abbreviations	v
1 Introduction	1
2 The Emergence of the Public Sector in Egyptian Cinema, 1957–1962	7
Historical Background: State Management of Cinema Affairs	8
Cinematic Awakening by Circumstance	10
CSI Established: Toward a Public Sector in Egyptian Cinema	13
CSI Reorganized: From a Cinema Supporter to a Film Co-Producer	19
Conclusion	24
3 The Expansion of the Public Sector in Egyptian Cinema, 1963–1966	25
Triggers for Change	25
The Birth of a New Era of State Involvement in the Film Industry	33
The Public Sector Expanded: To the Rescue	37
Conclusion	43
4 The End of the Public Sector in Egyptian Cinema, 1966–1971	45
A Struggling GEICRT: Between Inherent Problems, External Problems, and Unexpected Complications	46

The GEICRT Reorganized: Prevailing over Difficulties 56
On the Heels of the Defeat 62
The Dissolution of the GEIC 66

5 Conclusion 69

Appendix 73
References 79
About the Author 87

Abbreviations

CSI   Cinema Support Institution
GEIC   General Egyptian Institution for the Cinema
GEICRT General Egyptian Institution for Cinema, Radio, and Television
MCPAC   Misr Company for Performance Arts and the Cinema

CHAPTER 1

Introduction

Between an inevitable birth and a predestined death, historical inaccuracies and deterministic analyses prevail in the study of the public sector in Egyptian cinema, the outcome of which is none other than general confusion. Over four decades have passed since the dissolution of the General Egyptian Institution for the Cinema (al-Mu'assassa al-misriya al-'amma li-l-sinima) led to the unceremonious, perhaps premature, demise of public-sector film production in Egypt. Since that time, the Egyptian state's short-lived adventure in film production has sparked heated debate, attracting either mordant criticism or uncritical praise. Although a considerable volume of academic literature dealing with the Egyptian cinema has been published, little research has studied in depth the story of the public film sector in Egypt.[1] The first intention of this study is to fill this lacuna by shedding some light on the multilayered circumstances under which this sector emerged, expanded, and was eventually brought to an end.

What has been written about this sector takes the form of a few teleological interpretations, all yielding the same incomplete and somewhat distorted narrative that starts and ends with the assumption of inevitability. To many historians and film critics, the establishment of this sector was a foregone conclusion in a society experiencing an overall

---

1 A few exceptions include studies relating to the relationship between politics and cinema in Egypt in general, which more often than not devote a chapter or a section to the public sector in Egyptian cinema. Among these exceptions are Sharaffudin 2002; al-Nahas 2010; Abu Shadi 2000a; al-Tilimsani 1994.

drift to socialism, and they attribute its emergence mostly to a premeditated set of ideological elements.[2] The collapse of this sector, however, is strongly assumed by some scholars to have been predetermined by birth defects, namely, the absence of a clear ideological agenda.[3] From this frequently repeated narrative of the rise and fall of the public sector in Egyptian cinema, the sociopolitical and economic implications of contingent events, such as the Tripartite Aggression in 1956, the political tension between Egypt and some Arab countries from the late 1950s onward, the defeat of 1967, Nasser's death in 1970, and Sadat's Corrective Revolution, are typically excluded.[4] To propose a comprehensive and more accurate account of the public sector is, therefore, the second intention of this study, with a view to incorporating previously underplayed, seemingly unrelated influences into the analysis of the public sector's attitude toward the cinema.

This partial narrative is fueled by the political stances and backgrounds of the film critics concerned (al-Tilimsani 1995:70; Murad 1991:210). Writing in conformity with their times, which, more probably than not, were affected by the anti-Nasserist movement that ultimately aimed at "delegitimiz[ing] and demoniz[ing]" the Nasserist experiment,[5] critics were more inclined to assail the experience of the public sector in Egyptian cinema than to evaluate it. For most of them,

---

2 To mention only two: Hisham al-Nahas suggests that the state's decision to nationalize the Egyptian film industry came as a logical continuation of a decade-long wave of reforms, al-Nahas 1994:22–23; Ella Shohat explains how the creation of the public sector in cinema "was merely a continuation of the process of bureaucratically reshaping the state sectors along the lines of what was described as 'Arab Socialism,'" Shohat 1983:29.

3 Walter Armbrust and Fuad Mursi shed light on the issue of undercapitalization in Armbrust 1995 and Mursi, "al-Qita' al-'amm wa-l-istithmar al-khas," *al-Tali'a* 2 (February 1974):17. On bureaucracy and absence of a clear program see Gaffney 1987:59; Sharaffudin 2002:39, 71; and Muhammad Kamil al-Qalyubi, "al-Sinima al-misriya, da'irat al-hisar wa rihlat al-khurug," *al-Thaqafa al-Gadida*, 15 (1 January 1980):61.

4 Andrew Flibbert underlined this point in a personal correspondence with the author. Flibbert is an associate professor of political science at Trinity College, Connecticut, and the author of "State and Cinema in Pre-Revolutionary Egypt, 1927–1952" (Flibbert 2005) and *Commerce in Culture: States and Markets in the World Film Trade* (Flibbert 2007).

5 For a comprehensive definition of the anti-Nasserist movement, see Hatina 2004:102–104.

Introduction

the state's venture into film production is considered "the beginning of the 'setback' of Egyptian cinema" (Fayid in Gordon 2002:207) and they pejoratively brand this period "cinema of fear" (Sharaffudin in Gordon 2002:209). Moreover, they held the public sector accountable for the decline of Egyptian cinema, grounding their criticism in the manifold reorganizations that the public film companies underwent (Sharaffudin 2002:71; Mumtaz 1985:181). What these critics failed to see is what this study intends, in part at least, to highlight. Hence, the third and last main goal of this study is to suggest an alternative perspective, which, in lieu of dismissing these continuous structural organizations as weaknesses and failings, showcases them as an apparent indication of the state's resolve to reform and, in the process, rescue an industry in jeopardy.

This study also aims at rectifying the shortcomings in the existing literature. The constant lamenting of the public sector in Egyptian cinema automatically results in the dismissal of its films. Overwhelmed by preconceived notions, critics tend to overlook the great artistic value of some publicly produced films. A fact such as the Film Foundation's designation of *The Mummy*[6] (*al-Mummya'*, 1975) as "a gem of Egyptian cinema," and its subsequent selection to be restored, preserved, and screened at the Lumière 2015–Grand Lyon Film Festival goes unnoticed.[7] So does the fact that among the top 100 Arab films listed in *Cinema for Passion*, a book published by the Dubai International Film Festival in 2013, nine were produced by the public sector, with *The Mummy* ranking first and *The Land* (*al-Ard*, 1970) ranking fourth.[8] Even more, it seems as if the results of the referendum of 1995 conducted by the Cairo International Film Festival, which registered 30 public films among the top 101 Egyptian films produced between 1923 and 1995, are completely ignored by this scholarship, with the exception of the work of 'Ali Abu Shadi and Amal al-Gamal (Bahgat 1996:9–12).

---

6   Also known as *The Night of Counting the Years*.
7   The World Cinema Project is part of the Film Foundation, which was "created under the leadership of Martin Scorsese in 1990 to work for the preservation and restoration of heritage films." http://2015.festival-lumiere.org/en/program/the-film-foundation%27s-world-cinema-project.html (accessed on 17 April 2017).
8   Marwa Hamad, "Dubai International Film Festival Picks Top 100 Arab Films," *Gulf News*, 6 November 2013, http://gulfnews.com/leisure/movies/news/dubai-international-film-festival-picks-top-100-arab-films-1.1251874 (accessed on 10 March 2017).

In light of this, the importance of this study lies in the fact that it lays the foundation for an unprejudiced, more nuanced assessment of the public film sector. In so doing, the latter's role in introducing the possibility of "an alternative national cinema" (al-Tilimsani 1995:70) and as an incubator to "a new generation of talented filmmakers" (Gordon 2002:207) becomes evident.

The main body of this manuscript is divided into five chapters including the conclusion. Chapter two provides an introductory summary of the state involvement in Egyptian film industry from its inception in the early twentieth century until the Tripartite Aggression in 1956. The rest of the chapter examines the various factors that led to the emergence of the public sector in Egyptian cinema in 1957 and public-sector film production in 1960. The story continues in chapter three to tell how the ideological and economic repercussions of the sociopolitical transformations that Egypt witnessed between 1961 and 1962 drove the state to expand the public sector to encompass a considerable volume of film assets, without resorting to comprehensive nationalization. As a result, the state's film policy evolved from supervision and sponsorship to direct film production. Though this intervention succeeded in reviving a threatened film industry, rising difficulties necessitated a different film policy. The downsizing policy is, therefore, expansively discussed in chapter four, which also sheds light on the cinematic situation following the 1967 defeat. It is the author's contention that this policy, coupled with a new cinematic perception on the part of both the post-1967 government and the cineastes,[9] paved the way for the possibility of an alternative, critical national cinema, one that is politically charged and highly acclaimed. The story of the public sector ends shortly after the launching of the Corrective Movement in 1971, which caused the sudden end of this brief state adventure in film production.

In addition to a long list of secondary sources, this study relies heavily on several main sources. The official gazettes, *al-Garida al-rasmiya* and *al-Waqa'i' al-misriya*, proved essential in tracking the evolution and expansion of the public sector in Egyptian cinema, as they include all the presidential and ministerial decrees concerning cinema affairs. Another important source is the report of the Public Prosecution Office

---

9 The term 'cineaste' or 'cinéaste' may refer to an aficionado of filmmaking or any person associated professionally with filmmaking.

(al-Niyaba al-'amma) regarding the decade-long legal proceedings of the public film sector, which is absent from much of the existing literature. The National Charter of 1962, Nasser's speeches, and the 1968 Manifesto are also beneficial in constructing the historical context of the time period in which the public sector existed. The memoirs of Tharwat Okasha, which also include his correspondence and reports as the minister of culture, are consulted with the intention of viewing the story of this sector through the eyes of the state. Last but not least, the popular *Rose al-Yusuf* and the ideologically bound *al-Tali'a* are two contemporary periodicals that stand out as being of great value, including in their pages a wealth of information dealing with this sector as well as critical discussions of the role of the cinema.

This study focuses on the history of the public sector in Egyptian cinema as a state institution, and therefore intentionally avoids being caught up in the study of sociopolitical and cultural representations in Egyptian cinema. Viola Shafik's *Popular Egyptian Cinema: Gender, Class, and Nation*, Joel Gordon's *Revolutionary Melodrama: Popular Film and Civic Identity in Nasser's Egypt*, and Marisa Farugia's "The Plight of Women in Egyptian Cinema, 1940s–1960s" are only a few examples of the huge body of scholarship that deals with representations in Egyptian cinema. Film censorship is another topic that this study does not lengthily engage with, for censorship came in a variety of forms and agencies, not all of which operated under the purview of the public film sector.[10] The third trope that this study carefully avoids is the confusion between cinema matters and other communication media, particularly television and radio.[11] Except for a short period when all three media operated under the control of the same government authority, the public film sector was always regarded as a separate entity that had its own administration, budget, and policy.

A point should be made here: 'cinema' and 'film industry' are often used interchangeably when referring to the various institutions and

---

10 Except for the Artistic Censorship office that became a part of the Ministry of Culture in the late 1960s, but which was involved in examining the artistic level of a story or film rather than their political content.
11 Media such as television and radio are beyond the scope of this research. For a comprehensive understanding of the Egyptian media, see Armbrust 1996; Abu Lughod 2005; Boyd 1982; Boyd 1977; Diong 2015.

subsectors of filmmaking. The unit of analysis in this study is the public sector in the Egyptian cinema/film industry, which comprises governmental film organizations and state-owned companies that were involved in producing, distributing, and screening films. Also, it should be stated plainly here that establishing a public sector in cinema is different from launching a public-sector film production. Whereas the former entails the establishment of a state body charged to support (financially or technically), manage, and aid the cinema sector, the latter denotes the state's direct involvement in the film industry as a producer, distributor, and theater owner.

CHAPTER 2

The Emergence of the Public Sector in Egyptian Cinema, 1957–1962

From its inception in the early twentieth century, the Egyptian film industry depended solely upon private capital to finance its development and expansion. This private character of the film industry began to falter when the Egyptian government established the Cinema Support Institution (Mu'assassat da'm al-sinima) on 2 June 1957, officially marking the birth of the public sector in Egyptian cinema. Three years later, in 1960, the same institution acquired the necessary means to propel its venture into film production, signaling the emergence of public-sector film production in Egypt. By presenting a comprehensive and chronological assessment of the public sector in Egyptian cinema, this chapter attempts to propose a nuanced account of the circumstances under which public-sector film production came into being.

The chapter begins by briefly tracking the evolution of early Egyptian state involvement in the film industry, delineating the ways in which, from its origins, Egyptian cinema was regulated as part of a broader entertainment business, so lucrative that films were regarded primarily as economic commodities, whose 'sale' abroad added to the country's reserves of foreign currency. This perception of the cinema continued to prevail well after the 1952 revolution. Even though Egypt witnessed a kind of cinematic awakening on the heels of the Tripartite Aggression in 1956, it was mostly economic imperatives that drove the government to establish a public sector in Egyptian cinema. In time, and for considerations discussed below, the role of the state evolved from bureaucratic supervision of cinema affairs to actual film co-production. The nature of this involvement soon changed when the state, affected by a series of concomitant events, eventually adopted a more interventionist role in the film industry.

Historical Background: State Management of Cinema Affairs

Before delving into the historical roots of the public sector in Egyptian cinema, it is perhaps important to clarify that the Egyptian film industry was never entirely free of state meddling, the nature and extent of which have varied enormously over the years. To begin with, as early as 1911 the Cairo governorate dispatched officers to expurgate films that presumably threatened public order and morals, thus enforcing an ordinance that was not officially adopted by the central government until the introduction of censorship in 1914.[1] Almost a decade later, the Ministry of Finance passed a law regulating the import of foreign films, soon followed by a decree requiring close inspection by the Interior Ministry of Egyptian films destined for export (Abu Shadi 2004:45, 73; Wassef 1995:20). By 1930, the Ministry of Education had started producing short corporate films to promote Egyptian tourist attractions (Abu Shadi 2004:78). With a view to eradicating the illicit trade in film stock on the black market, a problem that surfaced after the Second World War, the Ministry of Social Affairs oversaw the distribution of such stock solely by authorized film companies (al-Sharqawi 1970:104–105). In 1947, the government felt compelled to establish the Chamber of the Film Industry (Ghurfat sina'at al-sinima) in reaction to another underlying problem that was seriously impairing Egypt's film production, namely, the lack of coordination between the three subsectors of filmmaking—production, distribution, and exhibition.[2] Though the coordination problems proved to be insoluble, the Chamber nevertheless succeeded in exerting a certain amount of control over

---

1 "Censorship," Alex Cinema, http://www.bibalex.org/alexcinema/industry/Censorship.html, accessed 30 November 2016; see also Thoraval 2000. For a fuller appreciation of film censorship in Egypt see Ali 2008 and Farid 2001b.
2 Andrew Flibbert explains this lack of coordination in Flibbert 2005:451–452. For more about the Chamber of the Film Industry, see Thabit 1994:1–37.

Historical Background: State Management of Cinema Affairs 9

cineastes by making Chamber membership mandatory for producers, distributors, and theater owners.

By the late 1940s, at least four ministries appeared to be involved in meddling in the film sector, which was frequently referred to at the time as "Egypt's second industry after cotton,"[3] probably in terms of export. Perhaps this explains why the Chamber of the Film Industry as a department came under the purview of the Ministry of Commerce and Industry, rather than a ministry of culture or guidance. This is not to suggest that the prerevolutionary state was unaware of the sociopolitical implications of cinema.[4] Rather, it appears as if it simply opted to overlook such considerations in favor of a more commercial stance. Even the censorship law of 1947,[5] naturally promulgated for broader media purposes, was mostly concerned with monitoring films, lest they contain material which could disturb the stability of Britain's colonial rule and Egyptian royalty, or lead to a boycott of Egyptian films anywhere abroad, but principally in sister Arab countries. Hitherto, state regulations, though limited and sporadic, had focused principally on handling economic issues affecting, and somewhat impeding, the development of what was largely perceived as a booming entertainment business. The end result of this attitude was, not surprisingly, the unintended rise of a commercial cinema brimming with romantic melodramas and

---

3   In his work on the economics of Egyptian cinema, Flibbert refers extensively to *Cine Film*, an Egyptian trade journal published continuously on a monthly basis between May 1948 and August 1960, in which there was regular mention of cinema being the second industry after cotton: Flibbert 2007. In their memorandum of 1952, the cineastes described the film industry as the third most profitable industry in Egypt. For a fuller appreciation of the memorandum, see Farid 1999:38–42.

4   The notion of cinema as a sociopolitical practice was not strange to the Egyptian art scene in the late 1940s. As early as 1947, Taha Hussein was introducing his readers to Jean-Paul Sartre's writings on the commitment of the artist, which he deemed useful for Arab artists. See, for example, Hussein 1947: 179.

5   The censorship law of 1947 was promulgated with the intention of prohibiting scenes projecting any negative image of Egypt or the Egyptian royalty. Chaotic events such as revolutions, strikes, and protests were not allowed to be represented in films. Nor could dirty alleys, donkey carts, and poor farm houses be depicted. "[F]ilmmakers could not: depict the power of God materialistically; represent religion in a disrespectful manner; use Qur'an or Bible verses in a comic fashion; attack any nation; undermine Egyptians or foreigners residing in Egypt; produce subjects or scenes of a bolshevist trait, or any propaganda against the monarchy or the government; and illustrate subjects or scenes that could lead to social disorders," Farugia 2002:48. See also al-Sharqawi 1966a:94; Abu Shadi 2000b:312; Farid 1995:107.

farcical comedies.[6] The shift in the perception of cinema from merely a hard-currency generator to a more powerful instrument of cultural enlightenment did not take place until years after the 1952 revolution.[7]

Cinematic Awakening by Circumstance

Hailing the cinema as an indispensable tool for education and influence, the Free Officers' figurehead leader, Muhammad Naguib, warned of the dreadful impact it could have if misused.[8] Shortly after the revolution, he called for a thorough transformation in filmmaking toward a more committed art, repudiating the decadent cinema of the past while encouraging the artists to "embed their mission in the [revolution]."[9] As a first step, the government permitted the public screening of previously prohibited films such as Fritz Kramp's *Lashin* (1938, starring Hasan 'Izzat and Nadya Nagi), Husayn Sudqi's *Down with Colonialism!* (*Yasqut al-isti'mar* [1952], starring Shadya, Husayn Sudqi, and Mahmud al-Miligi), and *Mustafa Kamil* (1953, starring Anwar Ahmad, Amina Rizq, and Magda).[10] Seizing the opportunity, Egyptian cineastes handed a memorandum to the general command of the armed forces in which they pushed for direct state support by means of bank loans, prizes, objective censorship, and institutional reorganizations (Farid 1999:38–42). The Chamber of the Film Industry also submitted a report to the Ministry of Commerce and Industry calling for an end

---

6 Of course, there were exceptions, but they were insufficient in number to be considered a collective cinematic movement. Kamal Salim's *The Will* (*al-'Azima*, 1939) and Kamil al-Tilimsani's *The Black Market* (*al-Suq al-sawda'*, 1945) are two early, prominent examples of Egyptian Realism. For more about these films, see Tawfik, n.d.:76 and Sharqawi 1970:78. In his memoirs, Tharwat Okasha imputed the existence of naive cinema to "money owners, foreigners, and Egyptianized citizens who had no purpose but profit-making." Okasha 2000:452.
7 Hamid Mowlana sheds light on a similar claim in his "Trends in Middle Eastern Societies" (Mowlana 1977:76). There he claims that among the factors responsible for the development of the cinema in Egypt is the state's interest in exploiting it as a source of hard-currency income as well as a tool of propaganda. Whereas I agree with him on the first, I disagree with him on the second. From the birth of Egyptian cinema and until years after the 1952 revolution, the Egyptian government did not show concrete interest in producing films for political or ideological purposes.
8 Muhammad Naguib's speech on 18 August 1952 as quoted in Gordon 2002:53.
9 'Abd al-Aziz 1975:142.
10 For a fuller appreciation of the post-revolutionary Egyptian cinema and its intersection with politics, see Gordon 2002.

to foreign film competition in local theaters.[11] This attempt to rescue the national film industry mostly from the control of foreign distributors and war-profiteers-turned-producers was reciprocated with a few, yet very pragmatic, governmental interventions. By imposing several different sets of taxes on imported films, replacing the severe censorship law of 1947 with a somewhat less restrictive, more general one,[12] reorganizing the Syndicate of Film Professions (Naqabat al-mihan al-sinima'iya),[13] and establishing the Fine Arts Department (Maslahat al-funun) in 1955, the state was still simply aiming to address inherent weaknesses in the management of the film industry.[14]

However, in the absence of a radical cultural transformation, and with a weak, if not absent, collective commitment on the part of cineastes, the Egyptian cinema remained subject to the mercy of the old profit-conscious mentalities, while the quality of films continued to deteriorate under the same market factors of the previous regime.[15] Thus far, cinema was first and foremost an economic commodity, with an almost exclusive emphasis on entertainment. To be sure, films inspired by the revolution started to emerge from 1954 onward, particularly ones condemning the previous monarchy and colonial rule, such as Ahmad Badrakhan's *God Is on Our Side* (*Allah ma'ana* [1955], starring Shukri Sarhan and Fatin Hamama) (Shohat 1983:29). Films showing realist features and addressing socioeconomic issues, like Salah Abu Sayf's *The Beast* (*al-Wahsh* [1954], starring Anwar Wagdi and Samya Gamal), Youssef Chahine's *Struggle in the Valley* (*Sira'fi-l-wadi* [1954], starring Farid Shawqi, Omar Sharif, and Fatin Hamama), and Tawfiq

---

11 By 1955, the Chamber was "claiming that producers and distributors had inadequate access to theaters for the first run of their pictures," Flibbert 2007:76; "It was said that Egyptian film production was crippled by the inability of Egyptian producers to wrest screen time from foreign films," Armbrust 2010:637.

12 Law no. 430 for 1955 canceled the previous censorship law of 1947 and replaced it with the following article: "protection of public morals, maintaining public order, and supreme state security," without any additional provisions. Abu Shadi 2000b:313; Farid 1995:108.

13 Law no. 152 for 1955 reorganized the Syndicate of Film Professions from a labor union to a professional one. Flibbert 2007:186; Farid 1999:38–42.

14 al-Sharqawi 1966b:61; 'Ali 2008:248. For a detailed chronological survey of laws concerning the film industry in Egypt, see Abu Shadi 1995:18–39.

15 Ella Shohat (1983:27) rightly argues that "although the revolution did not produce a complete transformation, it energized cultural life in Egypt."

12 The Emergence of the Public Sector in Egyptian Cinema, 1957–1962

Salih's *Fools' Alley* (*Darb al-mahabil* [1955], starring Shukri Sarhan) did appear; they were, however, the product of individual initiatives rather than collaborative, state-instigated efforts. The non-emergence of state-commissioned propaganda films during the first years of the revolution could be construed as an indication of the Free Officers' unpreparedness, and maybe indifference, to appreciate the political potential of the cinema.[16]

In fact, it was not until 1956 that the Egyptian authorities became aware of the powerful role that film—whether fiction or documentary—could play in mass mobilization. This sudden but tangible appreciation of the cinema as a propaganda tool came on the heels of the Tripartite Aggression, the invasion of Egypt by Israel, Britain, and France to regain Western control of the Suez Canal, when several short films and documentaries covering the events succeeded in galvanizing the Egyptian and regional public against blatant encroachments on Egyptian sovereignty, and by extension, support for the military junta's challenge to colonial hegemony.[17] Almost every other film produced after 1956 either had a protagonist who was an army officer, revolved around a patriotic theme, or idealized religious coexistence and solidarity among the Egyptian people.[18] It comes as no surprise that in the midst of this newfound cinematic sensibility, Badr Nash'at and Fathi Zaki co-authored a relatively progressive book entitled *Muhakamat al-film al-misri: 'ard wa naqd al-sinima al-misriya mundhu nash'atiha* (Egyptian Film on Trial: A Review and Critique of the Egyptian Cinema since Its Inception). In this work the two authors highlighted Vladimir Lenin's often quoted statement, "that of all the arts the most important for [a rising nation] is the cinema" (Nash'at and Zaki 1957). "[Egyptian] cinema," Ella Shohat writes, "became part of the initial stages of national

---

16 Baker 1974:395–397. Needless to say, many differences are apparent when comparing a political film commissioned by the state or promoting the state's ideology to a short promotional video produced by the Department of Information to mobilize the masses. While the first could be considered art, the second is dismissed as merely commercial advertisement.

17 *Let the World Witness* (*Fal-yashhad al-'alam*), an eight-minute film produced by the Art Department and directed by Sa'd Nadim in 1956. Abu Shadi 2000a:54.

18 For example, 'Izzaldin Dhulfiqar's *Give Me Back My Heart* (*Ruda qalbi*, 1957), whose premiere was attended by Nasser; Niyazi Mustafa's *The Prison of Abu Za'bal* (*Sign Abu Za'bal*, 1957); and Kamal al-Shaykh's *Land of Peace* (*Ard al-salam*, 1957); Shohat 1983:29–30.

building. . . . As a vehicle of the new ideology, [cinema] had the role of producing solidarity and identity among the masses" (Shohat 1983:28). In light of all the above, questioning the state's realization of how influential cinema could be becomes redundant. But whether the state had any intention to exploit the film industry to influence public opinion and mobilize the masses remains a question, which the following sections will attempt to answer.

CSI Established: Toward a Public Sector in Egyptian Cinema

It would be too simplistic to see the establishment of the Cinema Support Institution (Mu'assassat da'm al-sinima—hereafter CSI) on 2 June 1957 merely as a reflection of some sort of a cinematic awakening without giving any emphasis to the socioeconomic changes that nudged the government toward more interventionist measures. After the Tripartite Aggression, President Gamal 'Abd al-Nasser issued sequestration orders mainly against British and French nationals and many wealthy Jewish families, followed shortly by the Egyptianization decrees targeting foreign capital.[19] Along with the denaturalization law of 1956, not only did these orders alarm other foreign populations residing in Egypt, but they also affected them directly. Despite the reassurances given to these communities, many foreign residents, driven by fear of denaturalization, Egyptianization, and sequestration, left Egypt and relocated their businesses to other countries.[20] It is only plausible to assume that among the affected industries was the film industry, a large number of its shareholders being foreigners. Though there is no comprehensive record of these shareholders and the companies they owned, statistics show that the number of movie theaters and distribution houses plummeted after 1956, as did the number of imported and exported films.[21] The situation only got worse due to a shortage of imported European

---

19 For a fuller understanding of the economic situation in Egypt following the Suez Crisis, see Tignor 1998:114–192 and Waterbury 1983:57–103.
20 For example, American companies moved the seats of their Middle East operations to Beirut. Tignor 1998:140–141.
21 Ibrahim 'Umar, "Azmat al-sinima 3," *al-Ahram* 21030, 25 November 1971, 7; and *Arab Cinema and Culture, Round Table Conferences under the Auspices and with the Participation of the UNESCO* (Beirut: Arab Film and Television Centre, 1962), 76.

and American film stock.[22] In addition to the shortage in film stock, Egypt lacked the industrial know-how to manufacture cameras, projectors, and film printers. For these reasons, as Andrew Flibbert notes, "all parties appealed to the state for relief, demanding stricter regulation of the industry through a more comprehensive cinema law, with producers seeking greater controls on foreign imports" (Flibbert 2007:76). Not yet prepared to exploit the cinema, nor to anger the restive cineastes, but more importantly, unable to afford the loss of a great source of hard currency, the government felt it necessary to be more responsive and take measures to rescue an industry in dire need of assistance.

With the purpose of not only tackling these growing problems, but also enhancing the quality of Egyptian cinema and the country's national and regional cinematic standing, the Ministry of National Guidance sponsored the formation of the CSI, the first official cinema institution in Egypt as well as the Arab world.[23] Even though Fathi Radwan, then minister of national guidance, insisted that in order for the arts to serve the state, the latter should not intervene, the mere existence of the CSI anticipated the decision to place the industry under more governmental sponsorship and supervision (Abu Shadi 2000b:311).

The CSI was founded in accordance with, and made possible by, Law 32 of 1957 concerning public institutions, which, together with the Economic Institution (al-Mu'assassa al-iqtisadiya), spearheaded the expansion of the public sector in Egypt. With this in mind, it becomes plausible to assume that the creation of the CSI marked the emergence of a public sector in Egyptian cinema.[24] While a board of managers representing the Ministry of National Guidance and other Egyptian ministries determined production targets, the CSI had an independent budget raised from subsidies given by the state, tax revenues, or,

---

22 *Rose al-Yusuf* no. 1532, 21 October 1957, 30; to be clear, not all companies were 'Egyptianized.' "When officials of the Kodak Corporation inquired whether their firm would be required to Egyptianize because it imported only cameras and films, [Muhamad] Abu Nusayr [the Egyptian minister of commerce] replied that because the firm was not the sole importer of these products the law did not apply." Tignor 1998:141.
23 Presidential Decree no. 495 for 1957, *al-Waqa'i' al-misriya* 45, 6 June 1957, 9. See also al-Gamal 2009:25.
24 Almost six years before 1963—the often wrongly assigned birthdate of the public sector in Egyptian cinema.

as stipulated by Law 495, from Egyptian capital investment.[25] Among its objectives as a service sector, the CSI was to encourage both the screening of Egyptian films locally and the opening of new distribution markets abroad. It also aimed to secure bank guarantees and loans for producers in an effort to orient them toward the production of serious films that could reflect the state's general philosophy.[26] That same year, the CSI charter was declared by a presidential decree, stressing the need to raise the industry's professional and artistic level through various means, among which were eradicating the spread of exploitation within the film industry, cooperating and coordinating with the Fine Arts Department, and establishing a cinema studies institute.[27] Furthermore, subsidies were only to be given for the purposes of purchasing equipment, encouraging the production of ideological and educational films, and covering the financial losses of such films.

Irrespective of the circumstances leading to its formation, the establishment of the CSI marks a significant change in the state's cultural policy toward the film industry. In 1958 the newly created United Arab Republic underwent massive ministerial reorganizations whereby the Directorate of General Culture, previously belonging to the Ministry of Education, was annexed to the Ministry of Culture and National Guidance.[28] Under the auspices of the new minister Tharwat Okasha, a genuine advocate for the cultural role of the cinema, and with Naguib Mahfouz as its president, the CSI embarked on fulfilling the following long-term objectives. With the help of the Fine Arts Department, the CSI was able to send students to Russia, England, Italy, and Czechoslovakia to study filmmaking.[29] Furthermore, to ensure that funds did not fall into the wrong hands of "bankrupt parasites that ... could not care less about the arts," as stated by Yusuf al-Siba'i, then general secretary of the Higher Council for the Arts

---

25 Among the ministries were Education, Treasury, Social Affairs, and Labor.
26 Article 2 of Presidential Decree no. 495.
27 Issuance of the charter of the Cinema Support Institution, *al-Waqa'i'al-misriya* 78, 7 November 1957, 8–11.
28 Presidential Decree concerning the organization of the Ministry of National Guidance issued on 25 June 1958, *al-Garida al-rasmiya al-misriya* 17, 3 July 1958, 11; Presidential Decree concerning the Ministry of Culture and National Guidance issued on 26 June 1958, *al-Garida al-rasmiya al-misriya* 17, 3 July 1958, 13.
29 *Rose al-Yusuf* no. 1512, 3 June 1957, 29.

and Literature (al-Maglis al-a'la li ri'ayat al-funun wa-l-adab), the CSI secured loans only for producers and distributors whose project proposals were examined by the Fine Arts Department and deemed technically, artistically, and ideologically promising.[30] On top of that, applicants had to obtain at least one-third of the film's total budget in advance to be considered financially eligible for a loan.[31] Additionally, the CSI dispatched missions to explore potential markets in Latin America, India, and Indonesia, especially after some Arab and North African countries started banning Egyptian films owing to their presumed, or real, revolutionary content.[32] To ease the film stock crisis, shipments of film raw materials were sent to Egypt from the Eastern bloc.[33] Meanwhile, on the local front, and as an indication of the state's new outlook regarding the role of the cinema, censorship tax exemptions were granted to films imported by the Ministry of Culture and National Guidance for cultural and educational purposes (Flibbert 2007:108). In brief, the CSI did not aim to generate profit but to provide services and develop the film industry's infrastructure.

Notwithstanding these initiatives, the CSI failed to gain the unanimous support of the press, although it aroused a great commotion among the cineastes. Some journalists systematically described the failings of the CSI's general policy and urged the state to find long-term solutions instead of the temporary remedies that the CSI allegedly promoted.[34] Others directly accused its administration of abusing power

---

30 Article 24b of CSI Charter, *al-Waqa'i' al-misriya* 78, 7 November 1957, 10; it was reported in *Rose al-Yusuf* that any producer interested in applying for a loan from CSI had to have capital of at least LE 50,000, which pushed many producers to complain to Yusuf al-Siba'i that if they already had this amount, they would not need the loan in the first place. Al-Siba'i informed them that the full amount was not required if the project had prestigious names on board. Fathi Ghanim, "Yusuf al-Siba'i yudafi' 'an siyasat da'm al-sinima," *Rose al-Yusuf* no. 1522, 12 August 1957, 29.

31 Ghanim, "Yusuf al-Siba'i."

32 For a list of those missions, see al-Gamal 2009:28. As for the boycotting of Egyptian films, perhaps the first Arab country to do so was Libya. In the summer of 1957, the Libyan government banned the screening of Egyptian films such as *Suqut al-isti'mar*, *Mustafa Kamil*, *Allah ma'ana*, and *Port Sa'id*. *Rose al-Yusuf* no. 1522, 12 August 1957, 29.

33 *Rose al-Yusuf* no. 1532, 21 October 1957, 30.

34 Among these journalists is the well-known novelist Fathi Ghanim, who in his article "Mushkilat al-sinima" listed six long-term solutions that the film industry desperately needed. The CSI failed to adopt any of them. *Rose al-Yusuf* no. 525, 2 September 1957, 29.

CSI Established: Toward a Public Sector in Egyptian Cinema

and funds in favor of 'big names.'[35] Similar allegations were also made by a group of cineastes protesting particular acts of favoritism carried out by some CSI appointees.[36] According to the Syndicate of Film Professions, another body that claimed to be targeted by the CSI, its members were deliberately excluded from playing any role, temporary or permanent, in the CSI's formation, let alone its administration.[37] Adding fuel to the fire, Law 118 of 1958 removed a fundamental clause from Law 142 of 1955 that had made syndicate membership mandatory for anyone working in the film industry, even penalizing violators.[38] The ambiguity of both Article 8 and its supplementary note in the new law, which failed to define the boundaries of amateurism, provided all forms of 'amateurs' with a loophole to penetrate the film industry. Though this decree did not dissolve the syndicate, it certainly brought a storm of protest from its administration and members, for it incapacitated the syndicate and deprived it of whatever control it exerted over the cineastes. To be sure, it is extremely difficult to verify whether the state was intentionally targeting the syndicate to the advantage of the CSI, but so is the attempt to disprove such a claim. What is certain is that the decline of the Syndicate of Film Professions, which coincided with the faltering of the Chamber of the Film Industry, which by then had nominal powers only, resulted in the CSI practically becoming the sole public authority over cinema matters.

In spite of the syndicate's uproar, Egyptian cinema prospered in the late 1950s, in both quality and quantity. Although the CSI did not produce or co-produce any films in its early stages, it held film weeks in Cairo and selected Egyptian films to show in international film festivals. Toward the end of the decade, many books about cinematography

---

35 Nasir Husayn, "Kayfa nu'awid mu'assassat al-sinima ila da'm al-sinima al-'arabiya la al-agnabiya," *Rose al-Yusuf* no. 2245, 21 June 1971, 54–55.

36 For example, it was reported that Hasan Ramzi, who was on the committee in charge of establishing the CSI, started his own company shortly afterward to be able to take advantage of the benefits offered by the CSI. See "Yusuf al-Siba'i yarud 'ala thawrat al-sinima'iyin," *Rose al-Yusuf* no. 1529, 30 September 1957, 33.

37 *Rose al-Yusuf* no. 1528, 22 September 1957, 30; no. 1529, 30 September 1957, 33.

38 The article in question, concerning the reorganizations of the syndicates for the theater, cinema, and music professionals, stated that it is not mandatory for amateurs to join the Cineastes' Syndicate in order for them to work in the film industry. *al-Garida al-rasmiya al-misriya* 24A, 24 August 1958, 1–9. For the original text of the removed clause, see *Rose al-Yusuf* no. 2018, 13 February 1967, 35.

and cinema theory were translated into Arabic, and in late 1959, Egypt witnessed the establishment of the Higher Institute for the Cinema (al-Ma'had al-'ali li-l-sinima), the first institute to offer professional cinematic education in the Arab world.[39] The novelty of the institute lies in its diverse departments, which encompassed filmmaking, scriptwriting, editing, art direction, sound engineering, cinematography, and production. Moreover, permission for the creation of the Film Society (Gam'iyat film) was granted in hopes of holding regular cinema conferences and film screenings (Okasha 2000:454). As such, the CSI helped to create a nourishing atmosphere which allowed Egyptian cinema to "reach the peak of maturity and start being compared to [international cinemas]" (Farid 2001a:108). Highly acclaimed films such as Youssef Chahine's *Cairo Station* (*Bab al-hadid* [1958], starring Youssef Chahine, Farid Shawqi, and Hind Rustum), Henri Barakat's *The Nightingale's Prayer* (*Du'a' al-karawan* [1959], starring Fatin Hamama and Ahmad Mazhar), and Ahmad Diya' al-Din's *The Teenagers* (*al-Murahiqat* [1960], starring Magda and Rushdi Abaza) signaled the emergence of a new cinema, one with daring content and 'realist' tendencies.[40] What was regarded as the "marriage of literature and cinema" (Farugia 2002:53) also dominated during that period of time, manifested by the cinematic adaptation of novels by Naguib Mahfouz, Yusuf Idris, Ihsan 'Abd al-Qudus, and Tawfiq al-Hakim, all of which "reflected the problems and challenges of contemporary Egyptian life."[41]

The fact that the CSI did not yet commission the production of films might potentially be viewed as evidence of the state's sole interest in organizing the infrastructure of the film industry, rather

---

39 Classes started on 24 October 1959. See Mursi and Wahba 1973:74–75 and Qalyubi 1995:100.

40 The three films mentioned were submitted for consideration for the 31st, 32nd, and 33rd Academy Awards (Best Foreign Language Film) respectively, with *Cairo Station* being the first North African and Arab film to contend for the award. None were accepted as official nominees, however. They also participated in the 8th, 10th, and 11th Berlin International Film Festivals respectively.

41 This statement was made by critic Rafiq al-Sabban; see Joseph Fahim, "Arab Unity on the Silver Screen,"*Al Jazeera*, 4 April 2008, http://aljazeera.com/amp/focus/arabunity/2008/04/200852517281747506.html (accessed on 2 February 2017). Examples of these adaptations are 'Abd al-Qudus' *The Empty Pillow* (*al-Wisada al-khaliya*, 1957) and *Dead End* (*al-Tariq al-masdud*, 1958) and Naguib Mahfouz's *Beginning and End* (*Bidaya wa nihaya*, 1960) and *The Thief and the Dogs* (*al-Lis wa-l-kilab*, 1962).

than directly contributing to artistic or ideological film production. Another possible interpretation, however, is the comparatively neglected fact that up until 1960 the CSI did not have the necessary financial means to produce feature films, in particular since the lion's share of cinematic resources between 1957 and 1960 remained in private hands. Indeed, studios, distribution agencies, exhibition houses, and production companies were still owned by the private sector, the great generator of a commercial, politically detached cinema. The CSI was not financially strong enough to compete against private-sector film production, nor was fueling such competition considered a state priority. As a matter of fact, it was not until the sequestration of Bank Misr in 1960 that the state coincidentally found itself the owner of considerable film assets that would definitely facilitate its entry into the field of actual film production.

CSI Reorganized: From a Cinema Supporter to a Film Co-Producer

If economic necessities enabled the state to establish a public, largely supportive, sector in Egyptian cinema, financial convenience initiated the birth of public-sector film production in Egypt. In 1960, Nasser introduced Egypt's Second Five-Year Development Plan for 1960–1965, generally seeking progress on all economic fronts, including but not limited to a heavier industrialization program and the construction of the Aswan High Dam (Stephens 1971:356–377). In search of ways to finance such an extremely large-scale project, the Egyptian state turned its eyes toward private local capital, especially after repeated attempts to acquire sufficient foreign and joint capital proved a failure (Alexander 2005:123). To this end, Bank Misr was sequestered on 11 February 1960, as were all of its industrial and commercial subsidiaries,[42] among which, interestingly enough, was Misr Company for Performance Arts and the Cinema (Sharikat Misr li-l-tamthil wa-l-sinima—hereafter MCPAC), the parent company of the renowned Studio Misr (Hasan 1995:164). Taking into account firstly the LE 100 million of deposits that Bank Misr had, and secondly the paid-up capital of its 27

---

42 Presidential Decrees nos. 39 and 40 for 1960 concerning the ownership of Bank Misr and Bank al-Ahli respectively; *al-Garida al-rasmiya al-misriya* 36, 11 February 1960, 176–177.

enterprises which amounted to more than LE 20 million,[43] it is possible to claim that capital now became, in principle, available. That being said, it becomes conceivable to consider the acquisition of Studio Misr, along with its parent company, more an inadvertent by-product of broader financial objectives than a predetermined, comprehensive scheme.

Besides being the first and most prominent film studio in Egypt during that period, Studio Misr, like its contemporary counterparts, was a self-contained unit that incorporated four movie sets well equipped with lighting facilities, a black and white film laboratory, sound and camera equipment, and editing suites as well. Although in need of modernization and upgrade, it was capable of producing feature films. The significance of owning such a valuable cinematic asset did not go unnoticed by a state that during the preceding three years had been tirelessly trying to revive its film industry in all respects. Indeed, the Ministry of Culture and National Guidance secured a considerable budget "to develop ... and provide [Studio Misr] with modern sound equipment, cameras, and film-development factories, as well as processing apparatus for both color and black and white films" (Okasha 2000:454). It was around the same time that the state transferred the management of all its cinema-related affairs to the CSI, making the latter the executive director of the MCPAC and Studio Misr.[44]

A few months later, on 15 May 1960, Nasser signed a decree reorganizing the CSI by adding a new, essential clause that listed among the institution's main objectives the "production of films that are deemed necessary for national purposes or [crucial] in raising the level of Egyptian cinema."[45] Apart from this article and a few minor changes, the absence of any substantial difference between this decree and its predecessors might support the argument that only when the state acquired the appropriate cinematic assets did it really consider venturing into the field of film production. In any case, the decree certainly marks a shift in

---

43 These figures are taken from Waterbury 1983:72 and Tignor 1998:161. According to them, the Misr Group for Textiles (Misr Spinning and Weaving Company and Misr Fine Spinning and Weaving Company), for example, produced 60 percent of all textile production in Egypt.

44 Presidential Decree no. 93 for 1960 concerning management transfer from the directorate of cinema affairs in the Ministry of Culture and National Guidance to CSI.

45 Presidential Decree no. 855 for 1960 concerning the reorganization of CSI, Article 2, Section 3, Point 7; *al-Garida al-rasmiya al-misriya* 121, 28 May 1960, 846–848.

the government's role from a cautious cinema supporter to an enthusiastic, capable film producer. In this sense, Decree 855 of 1960 officially established public-sector film production in Egypt, almost three years after the establishment of a public sector in Egyptian cinema—not before and definitely not after, as it has been frequently argued.[46]

Despite having the means, it was too perilous to embark on an ambitious, solo journey to produce films when the state had no direct control whatsoever over the private sector, especially the distribution and exhibition agencies. The Ministry of Culture and National Guidance was extremely careful not to get caught up in the labyrinth of cinematic operations except for a few calculated steps (Okasha 2000:454). Over a period of three years, the CSI co-produced only three films. Although these were considered the state's first large-scale attempts at film propaganda, none of the three was instigated by the CSI. In comparison to the U.A.R. Radio Organization's annual budget, for example, the budget of the CSI was ridiculously small.[47] Given the financial and ideological attention that Nasser paid to the radio as a propaganda tool from the early years of the revolution, the huge difference between the radio's and CSI's budgets could perhaps reflect the fact that the Egyptian state was still hesitant to take the initiative to use the cinema as widely as radio and for similar ends. It is perhaps important to state here that in contrast to Sawt al-'Arab, a non-profit state agency established to communicate political messages to the Egyptians and the Arab world, the cinema sector, brimming with profit-oriented mentalities, was more difficult and more expensive to control and exploit.

O, Islam (*Wa-islamah*—also released as *Love and Faith*), directed by the Hungarian-American director Andrew Marton, appeared in 1961. It was the first Egyptian movie to be co-produced by the CSI, through the MCPAC, in cooperation with Ramsis Naguib's Arab Company for

---

46 See footnote 24. The establishment of public-sector film production in Egypt is wrongly assumed to coincide with the annexation of the CSI to the General Egyptian Institution for the Cinema, Radio, and Television in 1963, which in turn is incorrectly referred to as the onset of the nationalization of the film industry.

47 According to Okasha, CSI's budget for 1958–1959 was LE 241,300. It increased slightly to LE 300,000 in 1960–1961, only to decrease to LE 214,300 in 1961–1962. By contrast, the U.A.R Radio Organization's budget for 1960–1961 was LE 2,403,000, and LE 2,320,000 for 1961–1962. See the annual production budget as published in *al-Garida al-rasmiya al-misriya* 156, 13 July 1961, 941–978. Also see Okasha 2000:452–453.

the Cinema (al-Sharika al-arabiya li-l-sinima). Roughly around the same time, the famous actress-producer Asya Daghir, who was also the owner of the production house Lotus Film, requested a loan from the CSI to produce Youssef Chahine's *Saladin the Victorious* (*al-Nasir Salah al-Din*, 1963). Not only did the CSI accept, but it opted to become more involved by providing production facilities, namely services offered by Studio Misr.[48] In addition to meeting CSI's loan conditions and requirements, both of these epic historical films presumably contained features implicitly glorifying Nasser and his anticolonial message.[49] It is not possible to ignore the fact that these films were made at a time when relations between the U.A.R. and some other Arab states were growing increasingly bitter. While the fact that both films might have conveyed ideological sentiments probably encouraged the CSI to be a willing producer, having prestigious names on board—which naturally ensured low-risk investment and very high revenue—might have been the main clincher that persuaded it to finance and proceed with the co-production.[50] The third co-production was *It Happened in Egypt* (*Hadatha fi Misr*, 1963), this time with the Hungarian state-run company Hungaro,[51] probably in an effort to open international markets for Egyptian films.

At this point, a chain of concurrent events steered the Egyptian state toward a more interventionist policy, which ultimately catapulted the

---

48 The services provided for *Saladin the Victorious* by Studio Misr were sound recording and processing, as listed in the film credits.

49 To give an example of how film scholars perceived one of these films, see what Qussai Samak had to say about *Saladin the Victorious*: "Parallels were alluded to between the historical role of Saladin and the historical role of present-day Gamal 'Abd al-Nasser." Samak 1979:32.

50 Besides being produced by prominent producers as mentioned above, *O Islam* featured top-ranked actors such as Ahmad Mazhar, Lubna 'Abd al-'Aziz, Rushdi Abaza, Tahiya Kariyuka, Mahmud al-Miligi, Farid Shawqi, and many other Egyptian actors, as well as Europeans such as Luisa Mattioli, Folco Lulli, and Silvana Pampanini. *Saladin the Victorious* not only featured Ahmad Mazhar and Mahmud al-Miligi, but it was also directed by Youssef Chahine, adapted from Naguib Mahfouz's novel, and written by Yusuf al-Siba'i (plot) and 'Abd al-Rahman al-Sharqawi (script).

51 Not a lot of information is available concerning this film, its crew, and its cast. According to Samir Farid, it was screened in Hungary in 1963 but was not shown in Egypt until 1967. At first, it was supposed to be co-directed by the Hungarian filmmaker László Ranódy, but it was later assigned to his colleague Dola Mészáros, who co-directed it with Sayf al-Din Shawkat from Egypt. al-Gamal 2008:22.

CSI Reorganized: From a Cinema Supporter to a Film Co-Producer 23

various levels of the government into fast-paced socialism.[52] As a first measure, the socialist laws of July 1961 were introduced in three consecutive presidential decrees, targeting almost the whole private sector under the guise of "expanding capacities to support national interest."[53] What is surprising, however, is that aside from a small number of movie theaters, probably acquired incidentally as a result of the sequestrations of many holding companies, no major private film-related company was nationalized or sequestered so far.[54] Even more striking is the fact that when Nasser issued a decree concerning the redistribution of the 367 seized companies, only one company was listed under the CSI, the previously sequestered MCPAC (Abdel-Malek 1968:168–169).

Within a one-year period, the National Charter was declared, and even more drastic measures were taken in general.[55] Consequently, more sequestration orders were issued, ultimately affecting some shareholders of two of the biggest privately-owned film studios in Egypt, Studio al-Ahram and Studio Nahas (or Studio al-Nil).[56] Paradoxically, neither of these studios was put under the authority of the CSI. While the management of the former was transferred to the General Organization for Radio and Television (al-Hay'a al-'amma li-l-idha'a wa-l-talvizyun), the latter was brought under the supervision of the Sequestration Committee (Lagnat al-hirasa),[57] perhaps revealing the state's inability to

---

52 Among these events were the increasing difficulties with Syria, the growing tension between the old bourgeoisie and the new bureaucrats, the strong alliance between Egypt and the Soviet Union, and the crushing financial burden of the Five-Year Plan, as well as Egypt's intensified need for a self-reliant economy, and last but not least, the failure, or maybe reluctance, of the private sector to play a dynamic role in mobilizing the large amounts of capital required for the development plan. Johnson 1972:6–7; Abdel-Malek 1968.

53 Presidential Decrees nos. 117, 118, and 119 for 1961 concerning the nationalization of certain companies and institutions, buying shares from certain companies, and the special regulations of existing companies, respectively; *al-Garida al-rasmiya al-misriya* 162, 20 July 1961, 1046–1053.

54 Presidential Decrees nos. 117, 118, and 119. See also Waterbury 1983:76.

55 The National Charter was later misinterpreted and used by the private sector in Egyptian cinema to justify its existence and function. For an English translation of the National Charter, see Horton 1962.

56 Studio al-Ahram was established in 1945 by shareholders of various nationalities. To mention a few in alphabetical order: D. Akonomo, A. Attinogen, B. Bellini, A. Mukhtar, M. Shakir, M. Thabit, and S. Wissa. Studio Nahas was established in 1948 by Gabriel Edward Nahas, A. Khuri, and Yusuf Wahbi.

57 'Umar, "Azmat al-sinima 3," *al-Ahram* 21030, 25 November 1971, 7.

handle certain sequestered film properties. These random takeovers of cinematic assets might only reflect the lack of advance planning on the part of the Egyptian government. Moreover, the volume of these sequestered assets was too small to be viewed as an attempt at comprehensive film nationalization. In fact, the state showed little if any inclination toward nationalizing the film industry. In Okasha's words: "Until September 1962, when I left the ministry, there was no intention to nationalize the cinema nor [was the state] thinking of taking over cinematic production, for such a [step] entailed tumbling into countless problems with no sense of advance planning" (Okasha 2000:454–455). Clearly, for Nasser and his regime there were more pressing issues at stake than establishing a monopoly over the film industry.

Conclusion

To recapitulate, the establishment of the public sector in Egyptian cinema preceded the creation of public-sector film production. Whereas the former was the product of the government's response to both a new cinematic perception and economic imperatives, the latter was in a way the by-product of the sequestration of Bank Misr, which happened to be the holding company for the MCPAC, including Studio Misr. Both sectors, however, operated under the CSI's purview. Cinema remained primarily Egypt's "most popular form of urban entertainment" and the state acted with this in mind (Flibbert 2007:3, 48), giving the CSI the responsibility of keeping the film industry afloat, with a minor, yet growing, interest in the production of quality films. In fact, up to 1962, the successive waves of nationalization did not touch the film industry. Apart from coincidental sequestration of a few cinema-related assets, the state expressed little interest in embarking upon film production, limiting its involvement to sponsorship, supervision, financial aid, and occasional co-production ventures.

CHAPTER 3

The Expansion of the Public Sector in Egyptian Cinema, 1963–1966

Notwithstanding CSI's efforts to heal the Egyptian cinema from some of its particular ailments, the general sociopolitical and economic changes that Egypt experienced between July 1961 and September 1962 led to new complications, the ramifications of which heavily affected Egyptian cinema and the government's attitude to it. This chapter begins by contesting the prevailing misconceptions surrounding the expansion of public-sector film production in order to uncover the driving forces behind this development. The rest of the chapter addresses the evolution of the sector beginning in 1963, and ends with a survey of its manifold efforts to reinvigorate the film industry up to 1966.

Triggers for Change

Prevailing misconceptions. Perhaps the multiplicity of explanations surrounding the Egyptian government's resolution to expand public-sector film production is an indication of how multilayered the circumstances that led up to it really were. To some commentators, this expansion was inevitable in a society undergoing a general process of socialist transformation, mostly manifested by sequential waves of nationalization touching almost all sectors of the economy.[1] This argument is implausible, for it assumes that the expansion of the public sector was predetermined, an automatic result of decade-long historical developments. This theory will be repeatedly challenged in this work; the assumption of inevitability deliberately excludes other possibilities

---
1 For an example of these arguments, see chapter 1, note 2.

in our understanding of the public sector, mainly the impact of unexpected complications arising from unforeseen events.[2] Almost all of the state's decisions concerning cinema affairs, including the establishment of the CSI in 1957 and its reorganization in 1960, were not part of a preplanned, purely ideologically driven strategy, but rather pragmatic, somewhat experimental responses to the many ramifications of the ever-changing sociopolitical and economic realities that Egypt was witnessing at the time.

Other historians and film critics emphasize predetermined ideological factors in their analyses, which they ground in Nasser's declaration about the necessity of placing the intended Egyptian cultural revolution "at the service of the political and social revolution."[3] According to this view, in order to achieve the purpose of being "hostile to imperialism, hostile to feudalism, hostile to the domination and dictatorship of capitalism, hostile to all forms of exploitation" (Crabbs 1975:387), cinema ought to be brought under the wing of the state. To make this possible, as these scholars reasoned, the state had to nationalize the film industry and take control of its modes of production, but also its content and general philosophical assumptions, by means of a "socialism dictated from above,"[4] if not as "part of an overall plan to move Egyptian society in a new direction,"[5] then to freely "use the cinema as a propaganda tool" (Qalyubi 1980:61; see also Franken 1996:276). To challenge these arguments is difficult, for the cinema was indeed expected to play a role in conveying

---

2 The Tripartite Aggression in 1956, the dissolution of the U.A.R. in 1961, the Six-Day War and the defeat in 1967, Nasser's death in 1970, and the Corrective Revolution of 1971 were all unexpected events that gave birth to numerous complications affecting the whole economy of Egypt, including the film industry, which required prompt and pragmatic responses from the government.

3 See Nasser's speech on 28 December 1961 as cited in Crabbs 1975:387.

4 Shafik 2007a:20. See also Hasan 1995:164, in which the author argues that these developments fell in line with the prevailing socialist regime in an effort to put all the financial and artistic capacities at the service of the people. "State involvement, which culminated in 1961, took place in the context of Nasser's concern with the implementation of Arab socialism, which found its full expression in the 1962 Charter of National Action. This called for public ownership of much of the economy, control of all import trade and of three-quarters of the export trade." Malkmus and Armes 1991:51.

5 To be sure, Crabbs was speaking about the press among other sectors. Crabbs 1975:392.

ideological messages and promoting socialist philosophies. In the words of Salah Abu Sayf, the prominent film director who also happened to be the chairman of one of the public-sector film production companies:

> *Now that the revolution has expressed in the National Charter a global vision of history and of the future in a solid revolutionary context, it is imperative to [realize] how [feeble] our films are on the analytical and political level. It is now the task of the state to create, [on] the basis of the [National] Charter, a mature cinematographic world where man's struggle against fatal social conditions and his striving to change his destiny are expressed.*[6]

Nonetheless, all of these scholars base their analyses on the assumption that the film industry was nationalized. In so doing, they fail to realize that, unlike other Egyptian economic sectors, 'socializing' the film industry did not ensue from or require systematic nationalization, the centerpiece of Nasser's socialist agenda. To put it plainly, in order for a state to be able to control the modes of production of any industry, it has to either own or manage a significant volume of that industry's assets and personnel, monopolize the distribution of the product or the supply of raw material, or tighten its grip over the private sector. In the case of the film industry in Egypt, neither requisite was fulfilled. The state never showed any inclination to comprehensively control the film industry in its entirety, nor did it, except perhaps implicitly, target the film private sector, which continued to own the majority of cinematic resources.[7] Quite the contrary: the public sector was supposed to establish and maintain a trusting relationship with the private sector, to which, incidentally, it continued to provide services.[8]

---

6 As cited in Shafik 2007a:29. See also Abu Sayf 1965:93–96.
7 According to 'Abd al-Raziq Hasan, a professor of economics who was also the chairman of a public-sector film production company between 1966 and 1967, "people think the cinema in Egypt [was] nationalized, and this [was] not true ... more than sixty percent of the [cinematic] operations [were] not in the state's hands ... even the studios were not nationalized but bought." *Rose al-Yusuf* no. 2049, 18 September 1967, 25.
8 Interview with Salah Abu Sayf, *Rose al-Yusuf* no. 1804, 25 February 1963, 41; interview with Salah Amr, *Rose al-Yusuf* no. 1881, 29 June 1964, 42.

Perhaps the expansion of public-sector film production was somehow the outcome of a general drift toward socialism on the part of the government, but to cite ideological factors as the sole driving force behind such an expansion is simply misleading, if not erroneous. Besides, cinema was never the Egyptian government's preferred means of mass mobilization, not even the second. Before exploiting the cinema for its propagandistic potentials, the state had to first develop the infrastructure of the film industry to make it more accessible for a far wider audience. It made no sense for a state in times of economic and political turbulence to embark on a complex and expensive program of politicizing films that rarely reached rural areas and were, more often than not, banned in a number of Arab countries,[9] at a time when it had absolute control over the radio and television, which incidentally were much easier to manage, less costly, and more effective and far-reaching.[10]

Another reason for the presumed state takeover of the film industry was thought to be artistic and intellectual considerations. The film industry, it was claimed, was "drowning in the muddy waters of money, capitalism . . . and intellectual backwardness,"[11] forcing the state to intervene and prevent further artistic decline.[12] While it is somewhat plausible, this explanation is tainted by exaggeration. Although voices calling for better quality and more artistically oriented Egyptian films did arise, apparently they were not loud enough to drown out other concerns and convince Muhammad 'Abd al-Qadir Hatim, the new minister of culture and national guidance who was appointed in late 1962, and

---

9 According to a report by UNESCO, most of the exhibition houses were found in Cairo and Alexandria. The average rate of movie-going in Asyut and Giza was once a year, twice a year in Buheira and Sohag, and four times a year in al-Munufiya. As cited in Ibrahim 'Umar, "Azmat al-sinima 3," *al-Ahram* 21028, 23 November 1971, 7.

10 When the writer Ihsan 'Abd al-Qudus confronted the minister of culture and national guidance 'Abd al-Qadir Hatim about his preference for television over cinema, the latter denied it, but not before saying that it was much easier to make a new project successful than to fix the problems of an old one; *Rose al-Yusuf* no. 1809, 11 February 1963, 37. In another article, Hatim talked about the important role of television and radio in a socialist society without mentioning the cinema; 'Abd al-Qadir Hatim, "al-Idha'a wa-l-talvizyun fi-l-mugtama' al-ishtiraki," *al-Thaqafa* 52, 14 July 1964, 2–3.

11 *Rose al-Yusuf* no. 1914, 15 February 1964, 44.

12 As stated by Ihsan 'Abd al-Qudus in *Rose al-Yusuf* no. 1874, 11 May 1964, 44.

other cineastes to perceive film primarily as an art form.[13] Even after the expansion of public-sector film production, discussed in the following sections, filmmaking was still expected to be profitable and cinema never ceased to be regarded as, above all, a profit-making entertainment business. A necessary expectation of any film produced by the public sector was, as a minimum, to cover its costs of production.[14] To be sure, the leadership of the public sector did favor films with a socialist drift and certain aesthetic standards; nevertheless, there was never any doubt about this sector's additional, but equally crucial, *raison d'être*—potentially contributing to national economic development.[15]

By emphasizing only the aforementioned powerful ideological or artistic factors in their analyses of the expansion of the public sector, these historians and film critics tended to overlook, or perhaps ignore, the significant role of other key elements. For reasons discussed below, it is possible instead to view economic imperatives as a central propelling factor behind the state's inclination for more involvement in cinema affairs.

Economic imperatives: At the heart of change. To begin with, political tension between Egypt and neighboring countries started to grow in the early 1960s. Iraq was the first Arab country to ban the importation of Egyptian films, followed shortly by Syria after the dissolution of the U.A.R.[16] This practice of boycotting Egyptian cinema spread to other countries when the governments of Jordan, Tunisia, and Morocco, deeply concerned about the implicit political content that some Egyptian films might contain, followed suit.[17] As a result, the number of exported copies of Egyptian films dropped from 1,115 in 1959 to 744 in 1963 (Qalyubi 1980:61–62). Because 60 percent of the Egyptian film industry's revenues came in hard currency from the Arab markets, this ban naturally had a dramatic

---

13 Munir 'Amr, "Awal duktura fi-l-sinima," *Rose al-Yusuf* no. 2069, 5 February 1968, 66. See also al-'Ashari 1968.

14 Nasir Husayn, interview with Salah Abu Sayf, *Rose al-Yusuf* no. 1809, 11 February 1963, 38.

15 Article 3 of Decree no. 48 for 1963 concerning the organization of the GEICRT, *al-Garida al-rasmiya al-misriya* 7, 8 January 1963, 14.

16 'Abd al-Fatah Fishawi, "La sira' bayna al-aflam al-misriya wa-l-aflam al-lubnaniya," *al-Kawakib*, 12 July 1966, 17; al-Gamal 2009:27.

17 *Rose al-Yusuf* no. 1931, 14 June 1965, 46; Murad 1991:205–207; Gaffney 1987:60.

impact on the film distribution sector in Egypt.[18] Driven by fear of inevitable bankruptcy, a large number of foreign and Egyptian distributors shut down their offices in Egypt and relocated to Beirut, making the latter, though for a very short period of time, the distribution hub of the Middle East.[19] The direct repercussion of these relocations was unmistakably a diminishing cash flow that limited the amount of capital available for distribution advances, the oldest and most common method of funding film production in Egypt. Prior to filming, producers relied heavily on cash subsidies provided by distributors with the stipulation that all these advances would later be reimbursed from the film's revenues; otherwise the film's copyright ownership would remain in the hands of the distributor (Thabit 1994:27–30). This was a formula that not only empowered the distribution sector at the expense of other sectors, it also held the economic development of the film industry hostage to the big distribution networks, the end result being that Egyptian cineastes were placed at the mercy of businessmen.

Another victim of these changing circumstances was the exhibition sector, for distributors were also in charge of importing foreign films and selling them to theater owners. When these distribution companies relocated, the least fortunate theater owners lost their main suppliers, finding themselves short of material to screen, and before long out of business.[20] Others, who were audacious enough, or maybe desperate enough, to defy the law, resorted to illegal means

---

18 Dajani 1980:91–92; Okasha 2000:767; Fatin 'Abd al-Wahab, proceedings of *Arba' mu'tamarat*, 12–13 October 1966, *al-Kawakib*, 25 October 1966, 30–35. See also Mahfouz 1995:127.

19 "The efflorescence of Lebanese commercial production occurred when the Egyptian public sector was at its peak. . . . It was still possible to produce privately financed films in Egypt, but much of the capital that had previously financed Egyptian cinema nonetheless went to Beirut." Armbrust 2010:633–634. This 'emigration' phenomenon would last for years after the establishment of the GEICRT. See Nasir Husayn, "Harb al-a'sab dud al-sinima al-misriya," *Rose al-Yusuf* no. 2021, 6 March 1967, 34. Naguib Mahfouz addressed this issue in his testimony in "al-Nas al-kamil li taqrir al-niyaba al-'amma bi hafz al-tahqiq fi qadiyat khasa'ir al-qita' al-'amm al-sinima'i fi Misr," *al-Sinima wa-l-tarikh* 7 (1993): 80.

20 The number of movie theaters plummeted from 450 in 1955 to 350 in 1962. Obviously, Egypt was suffering from a severe shortage of theaters. *Arab Cinema and Culture*, 73.

Triggers for Change 31

of trade such as smuggling films in and out of Egypt to keep their businesses running,[21] potentially causing the state to lose a hefty sum in tax revenues from film importation and exportation. Furthermore, television was introduced in Egypt in 1960, immediately becoming the primary source of family entertainment. As a result, movie attendance dropped dramatically from 1960 onward, negatively affecting the exhibition sector, which plummeted from 400 cinema houses in 1960 to 298 in 1963 (Mahfouz 1995:126–128). Within a one-year period between 1961 and 1962, the subsectors of the Egyptian film industry, like a falling row of dominos, crumpled one after another. As the volume of exhibition houses shrank and the number of moviegoers decreased (and vice versa), the less profitable the films became and the fewer funds invested, leading to a considerable stagnation in film production.[22]

Many of those who were not affected by the lack of cash flow but alarmed by the colossal political changes in the country rushed to liquidate their assets for fear that they would be sequestered,[23] while others prospered in the absence of competition, thus succeeding in establishing a quasi-monopoly over continuing, but anemic, film production. This kind of control aimed first and foremost to garner commercial success, encouraging the expansion of an existing star system, which entailed the selection of only famous actors and directors and conventional plots. Consequently, less-known cineastes, who formed the majority of film professionals, found it difficult to get decent work,[24] eventually leading to another wave of cineastes fleeing the country, seeking opportunities abroad.[25]

As a result of all these transformations, the Egyptian film industry found itself suffering its worst recession since its inception in the

---

21 Nasir Husayn, "Limadha umimat sharikat al-tawzi'," *Rose al-Yusuf* no. 1869, 6 April 1964, 44.
22 To follow the production rate in the Egyptian film industry across various years, see Flibbert 2007:47, fig. 3.3.
23 Among the factors that facilitated the state's takeover of some film companies was the owners' willingness to sell and leave before having their properties sequestered. See Okasha 2000:756; al-Nahas 1994:22.
24 For more about the star system in Egypt, see Ayad 1995:134–137; Malkmus 1988:31; 'Abd al-Aziz 1975:140–142.
25 *Rose al-Yusuf* no. 2021, 6 March 1967, 34.

early twentieth century, pushing the cineastes to raise their voices in protest.[26] While some sought help from the state in hopes of sparing the national film industry more humiliation and degeneration, others, it was claimed, had ulterior, and somewhat more personal, motives for exhorting the state to interfere (Okasha 2000:756; Nahas 1994:22). The film companies that the state took over were those that were no longer making a profit or were drowning in debt, thus providing them with a convenient opportunity to escape monetary burdens.[27] The state listened to these restive voices, but what encouraged it to oblige was its own interest in having a thriving film industry. On top of all the pressing issues that were at stake at the time, it was obvious that the Egyptian government could not afford to lose another source of income. Previous policies of supervision and sponsorship were no longer tenable. The government felt it necessary to take more drastic measures to expand its control over the various modes of production, with a view to getting the stagnant film industry moving.

A particular point should be made here: by fostering such an extremely interventionist film policy, the state was to a certain extent trying to save face. A rising socialist regime promising in its National Charter to offer all of its citizens "the right to secure the job that suits educational background, abilities, and interests" (Horton 1962:16) could not possibly have tolerated a relatively high rate of unemployment in any industry, let alone the film industry.[28] Even more to the point, at the base of both the socialist laws of 1961 and the National Charter of May 1962 was an urge to reclaim the forces of production from "parasitic exploitation," which probably pushed the government to find new means to secure enough cash flow to liberate the film industry from the control of the large private companies.[29] For all of these reasons, the state expanded the public sector in Egyptian

---

26 "Al-Sinima al-misriya fi khatar," *al-Hilal* 10, 1 October 1967, 113–114.

27 Okasha argues that some cineastes wanted the state to take over film production and exerted pressure in this direction: Okasha 2000:756.

28 See what Salah Abu Sayf had to say about the emigration of the cineastes and the high unemployment rate in his testimony in "al-Nas al-kamil li taqrir al-niyaba," 86.

29 For example, the largest chain of movie theaters was owned by Elias Georges Lutfi, who owned 26 cinemas in Cairo and Alexandria. The second largest was controlled by the Eastern Company for the Cinema. See Flibbert 2007:187.

cinema, becoming a producer, a distributor, an exhibitor, and sometimes a spectator as well.[30]

The Birth of a New Era of State Involvement in the Film Industry

"But control over all the tools of production does not mean the nationalization of all the means of production, the abolition of private ownership, or interference with the rights of inheritance" (Horton 1962:13).

Thus spoke President Nasser in May 1962 as he discussed the National Charter of the U.A.R. Indeed, by establishing the General Egyptian Institution for Cinema, Radio, and Television (al-Mu'assassa al-misriya al-'amma li-l-sinima wa-l-idha'a wa-l-talvizyun, hereafter GEICRT) on 6 January 1963,[31] the state was seeking to claim considerable control of the film industry's modes of production with a view to reinvigorating an industry in jeopardy, rather than nationalizing it in its entirety.[32] Before embarking on the story of the GEICRT, it should once again be stated plainly that the film industry, as it existed, was not nationalized in 1963, contrary to oft-repeated claims. To be absolutely clear, the Egyptian government never established a complete control of all aspects of filmmaking, nor did it have any intention to do so in the first place; the orders for sequestration of cinema-related assets were too sporadic and unplanned to imply the existence of an ideologically motivated state strategy aimed at comprehensively nationalizing all the various sectors of the national film industry. Moreover, throughout the public sector's experiment, the volume of state-owned and state-managed properties did not exceed 30 percent of all Egyptian cinematic assets, the rest remaining in

---

30 Tawfiq Salih stated in an interview that "the revolution did not only give financial aids, but also [used to] fill the theaters with soldiers twice a week." Murad 1991:204.
31 Decree no. 48 for 1963 concerning the organization of the General Egyptian Institution for the Cinema, Radio, and Television, *al-Garida al-rasmiya al-misriya* 7, 8 January 1963, 13–16.
32 In his testimony during the trial of the public sector in Egyptian cinema that took place in the early 1980s, Salah 'Amr, the chairperson of the sector between 1963 and 1966, repeatedly reiterated that public-sector film production came into being only to save an industry on the verge of collapse. See "al-Nas al-kamil li taqrir al-niyaba," 83.

private hands.³³ A more accurate version of what took place as of 6 January 1963, the presumed birthdate of film 'nationalization' in Egypt, will reveal how a relatively modest public, and in so many ways experimental, institution known as the CSI was merely expanded into the GEICRT, another public institution but one in charge of three different means of mass communication, of which cinema was perhaps the junior partner.³⁴ Because radio and television matters fall outside the scope of this study, only decisions governing cinema affairs will be analyzed.

Unlike the socialist laws of July 1961, Decree 48 of 1963 creating the GEICRT did not employ the usual terms of 'nationalization,' 'sequestration,' 'expropriation,' or 'confiscation'; instead the key term used was the somewhat benign 'incorporation' (*indimag*) of the CSI into the GEICRT.³⁵ Nevertheless, maintaining that the terms employed did not evoke any form of nationalization should not undermine GEICRT's distinctiveness, nor negate the fact that it inaugurated a new and vigorous stage of state involvement in the film industry.

Though very analogous in outer form and administrative structure, a closer examination would reveal that not only did the CSI and the GEICRT differ in essence, but also their *raisons d'être* were on opposite ends of the scale. To begin with the essential similarities, in their quest to raise artistic and professional cinematic standards, encourage

---

33 Based on numbers provided by many sources, the total number of films produced by the public sector did not amount to more than 40 percent of the total number of all films produced in Egypt during the same period. See Abu Shadi 2000b:322–324; Tharwat Okasha's report to the Speaker of the Egyptian Parliament on 15 April 1972, published under the title "al-Qita' al-'amm al-sinima'i fi Misr," in the archives section in *al-Sinima wa-l-Tarikh* 8 (1993); and a personal document provided by the Rare Books and Special Collections Library at the American University in Cairo listing all the films produced between 1951 and 1970. According to a table created by Andrew Flibbert based on numbers provided by the Central Agency for Public Mobilization and Statistics and *al-Sinima wa-l-masrah* (Flibbert 2007:188), the size of the public exhibition sector did not exceed one-fourth of the whole exhibition sector in Egypt.

34 Decree no. 48, *al-Garida al-rasmiya al-misriya* 7, 8 January 1963, 13–16.

35 Article 1, *al-Garida al-rasmiya al-misriya* 7, 8 January 1963, 14. Almost every scholarly work examining the history of Egyptian cinema refers to what took place in January 1963 as the onset of film nationalization in Egypt. The exceptions, 'Ali Abu Shadi and Andrew Flibbert, are perhaps the only ones to use the most accurate terms—'incorporation' or 'consolidation'—to describe the development in question. See Flibbert 2007:108; Abu Shadi 2004:181.

the exhibition of Egyptian films at home and abroad, and secure loans, financial aid, and offer prizes for serious projects, the GEICRT and the CSI were identical.[36] Both, indeed, came into being at a time when the film industry was in dire need of assistance. As for the differences, while the CSI's rules predicated the receipt of financial aid on the production of films that "fall in line with the state planning policy,"[37] GEICRT's regulations closely linked its annual production plan with the laws of supply and demand.[38] Clearly, economic considerations played a decisive role in Egypt's film policy, much to the chagrin of the former minister of culture and national guidance, Tharwat Okasha, who viewed the cinema primarily as belonging to the cultural sphere and warned of the dreadful impact that would result from subjecting art to business or ideological considerations, as it appeared to be the case for radio and television.[39] This particular understanding of the role of the cinema was not shared by the succeeding minister, Muhammad 'Abd al-Qadir Hatim, which might explain, to some degree, this shift in the ministry's film policy under the latter's supervision. In fact, under Hatim, the GEICRT was to become an institution devoted to financial concerns,[40] not the least of which was the requirement that the GEICRT should generate enough income to cover expenses and capital costs,[41] a

---

36 Articles 2 and 6, Decree no. 495 for 1957 concerning the establishment of CSI, *al-Waqa'i' al-misriya* 45, 6 June 1957, 9; Article 2 of Decree no. 855 for 1960 concerning the reorganization of CSI, *al-Garida al-rasmiya al-misriya* 121, 28 May 1960, 846; and Article 3 of Decree no. 48 for 1963 concerning the organization of GEICRT, *al-Garida al-rasmiya al-misriya* 7, 8 January 1963, 14.

37 Article 2, clauses 3 and 8, Decree no. 855 for 1960 concerning the reorganization of CSI, *al-Garida al-rasmiya al-misriya* 121, 28 May 1960, 846.

38 Article 8, clause 1, Decree no. 48 for 1963, *al-Garida al-rasmiya al-misriya* 7, 8 January 1963, 15.

39 Okasha seems to disapprove of the incorporation of the CSI into the GEICRT; he thought such a step would only confuse the mission of art and culture with that of proper media. Okasha 2000:662, 756.

40 Article 1, Decree no. 48, *al-Garida al-rasmiya al-misriya* 7, 8 January 1963, 14.

41 Law no. 256 for 1960 concerning the organization of public institutions of an economic nature; see also Hilmi Hilal and Nasir Husayn, "Hal tadkhul al-sinima magganan," *Rose al-Yusuf* no. 2020, 27 February 1967, 36–37. In his article, the journalist Gamil al-Baguri quoted Naguib Mahfouz, referring to the GEICRT as an "institution with an economic aspect that aim[ed] not only to [provide services] but to make a profit." *Rose al-Yusuf* no. 1878, 23 March 1964, 44–45. Despite this, the GEICRT continued to be a financial burden on the state. More will be said about this issue in the following chapter.

stipulation that was overlooked later on. Moreover, by providing it with a separate "juridical personality,"[42] the Egyptian government bestowed on the GEICRT the right to instigate litigation, enter contracts, incur debts, sign agreements, and own property.[43] The flip side of this arrangement was that the state could no longer shield the GEICRT from legal liability, making the latter susceptible to lawsuits.[44] As a consequence, in theory at least, the GEICRT was no longer a non-profit public service institution, financially dependent on or legally protected by the state as the CSI had been. Instead it was an institution in which fiscal responsibility was the highest concern. Although still a public body and answering to the same higher authority as before, it operated as an autonomous holding company that was meant to run strictly along economic lines (Wahba 1972:32).

What markedly differentiated the GEICRT from the CSI was the former's wide range of capacities, allowing it to "execute industrial and commercial projects . . . , initiating commercial distribution of its products [as well as products of other companies]," and "establishing, buying, exploiting, or renting studios and exhibition houses." Combined together, these newly introduced provisions marked more direct state involvement, gradually fostering an omnipresent, expansionist state role in film industry. From merely a supporter of a non-profit-seeking film industry, the GEICRT deliberately and self-consciously became a key film producer aiming at exploiting revenues to finance further projects. In this sense, it becomes possible to view the emergence of the GEICRT, in light of its recent financial structure and constraints, not as a logical continuation of previous cinematic trends, but rather as a breakaway from existing operating patterns.

In line with this change of priorities went a change of funding sources and modes of production. In the hopes of arming itself with

---

42 Article 1, Decree no. 48, *al-Garida al-rasmiya al-misriya* 7, 8 January 1963, 14.

43 See Articles 52–53 concerning the juridical personality in the second chapter of the Egyptian Civil Code, which was promulgated by Law no. 131 of 1948 (personal copy). In his book *The Law of the United Nations: A Critical Analysis of Its Fundamental Problems*, Hans Kelsen states that "juridical personality means the capacity of being a subject of legal duties and legal rights, of performing legal transactions and of suing and being sued at law" (Kelsen 1964:329).

44 A detail that would allow the instigation of a decade-long lawsuit against the public sector, as discussed in the conclusion of this study.

the appropriate means to achieve the highly ambitious and costly objectives mentioned above, the GEICRT was to exploit the capital of the MCPAC and Studio Misr, along with other companies that were to be determined by a presidential decree.[45] With this power vested in it, the GEICRT was able to dissolve and liquidate the MCPAC and replace it with other companies, each of which was given a distinct mission (Okasha, "Qita' al-'amm," 6). In a matter of a few weeks, the GEICRT had become a bureaucratically run, vertically integrated film production company, not only capable of producing, distributing, and exhibiting films, but enthusiastically willing to plunge into the murky field of film production. Okasha's memoirs paint this as a long leap forward beyond the state's initial and cautious plan for the cinema.

From an attempt to raise the status of the cinema whilst still in the hands of its private owners and without any direct interference from the state, except for the occasional participation in co-production or the production of a small number of good quality films, the plan changed upside down to constitute [direct involvement] in production, distribution, and exhibition; this philosophy [was] completely different from what I had envisioned in this respect.
(Okasha 2000:455)

Thus when Decree 48 of 1963 was announced, it came as a surprise, for it was not in consonance with previous state film policies represented by the CSI, which had limited its role to encouraging sponsorship and participating in carefully selected co-production projects. Even more, the hasty manner in which the GEICRT was established manifested a sense of urgency on the part of the Egyptian government.

The Public Sector Expanded: To the Rescue
On 14 January 1963, only eight days after the establishment of the GEICRT, its board of directors, chaired by Salah 'Amr and with Naguib

---

45 Article 4, clauses b and e. Decree no. 48, *al-Garida al-rasmiya al-misriya* 7, 8 January 1963, 14.

Mahfouz and director Ahmad Badrakhan as its consultants,[46] oversaw the creation of four separate companies. With the intention of producing feature films, the General Company for Arab Film Production–Filmontage (al-Sharika al-'amma li-l-intag al-sinima'i al-'arabi) was created, operating under the supervision of filmmakers Salah Abu Sayf and Hilmi Rafla. As for the business of co-production, the GEICRT established the General Company for International Film Production–Coprofilm (al-Sharika al-'amma li-l-intag al-sinima'i al-'alami), whose chairman, Muhammad Tayfur, shortly announced its primary objective—attracting the attention of great international film producers.[47] Right after their establishment, both Filmontage and Coprofilm eagerly confronted such issues as the unemployment and relocation of film professionals by employing as many professionals as possible, purchasing scripts and film plots to be adapted for the big screen, and signing numerous film deals with cineastes from the private sector with a view to starting early production.[48]

The third company to be created by the GEICRT was the General Company for Studios (al-Sharika al-'amma li-l-studiuhat), whose responsibility was to run Studio Misr, developing the infrastructure of the old studios as well as buying and building new ones. In addition to acquiring Studio Misr and Studio al-Ahram, the General Company for Studios purchased Studio Galal from the actress-producer Mary Quiny and Studio Nahas from the relevant sequestration committee.[49] Furthermore, in response to the cineastes' complaints about high production costs, the rising prices of film stock, the increase in movie-set rents, and the lack of sound tapes and special lighting equipment,[50]

---

46 From 1963 to 1966, the chairman of the GEICRT was the engineer Salah 'Amr, who is regarded as the father of broadcast engineering in Egypt. Among the board members were Naguib Mahfouz and the well-known director Ahmad Badrakhan, both of whom held the post of consultant. For a full list of the GEICRT's board members, see Decree no. 49 for 1963 concerning the formation of the GEICRT's board of directors, *al-Garida al-rasmiya al-misriya* 7, 8 January 1963, 16.

47 The co-production phenomenon between Egypt and other countries emerged years before the public sector, in 1948, and was acclaimed as a great generator of income. See al-Gamal 2009 for a comprehensive investigation of co-production.

48 *Rose al-Yusuf* no. 1808, 4 February 1963, 42; Farid 1973. See also the testimonies of Fahmi 'Ali Hasan, a member of the financial committee that evaluated the public sector, and Salah Abu Sayf in "al-Nas al-kamil li taqrir al-niyaba," 78, 86–87.

49 Ibrahim 'Umar, "Azmat al-sinima 3," *al-Ahram* 21030, 25 November 1971, 7.

50 *Rose al-Yusuf* no. 1937, 26 July 1965, 59; no. 1938, 2 August 1965, 46–47.

the cornerstone of a new 'Cinema City' was laid by 'Abd al-Qadir Hatim in Giza as compensation. The resources included studios and factories, mostly to start manufacturing cinematic equipment and raw material locally, and partly to attract international directors and producers to choose Egypt as their films' set location.[51]

Finally, the GEICRT established the General Company for Film Distribution and Exhibition (al-Sharika al-'amma li tawzi' wa 'ard al-aflam) to supervise the purchase and construction of new movie theaters (Okasha, "al-Qita' al-'amm," 4; Abu Shadi 2004:182). As a first measure, the state transferred the management of previously sequestered exhibition houses to the General Company for Film Distribution and Exhibition.[52] This company, it was suggested, allegedly intended to construct 4,000 movie theaters, one for every village, in an effort to "generalize socialist entertainment and culture" (Mahfouz 1995:127). This figure is most probably an exercise in exaggeration attesting to the GEICRT's over-enthusiasm rather than a building program that it actually meant to fulfill. Indeed, at that stage, the GEICRT can be criticized only for being too ambitious, almost blinded by its own tunnel vision.

As a result of these actions, the total amount of salaries paid out to the GEICRT's employees increased from LE 29,000 in 1962 to LE 118,000 in 1963, and, if Okasha is to be believed, to LE 1,939,000 in 1964.[53] Without dismissing Okasha's figures as farfetched, this huge rise of salaries would be plausible only if they also included the wages paid to actors, directors, scriptwriters, and other film professionals commissioned by the GEICRT on a contractual basis. In any case, the GEICRT succeeded in reviving the film industry, avoiding the escalation of one adverse situation—unemployment

---

51 *Rose al-Yusuf* 1931, 14 June 1965, 46; Okasha 2000:757; Nasir Husayn, "Kayfa nu'awid muassasat al-sinima ila da'm al-sinima al-'arabiya la al-agnabiya," *Rose al-Yusuf* no. 2245, 21 June 1971, 54–55.

52 Abu Shadi 2004:182. For a list of the 298 movie theaters in Egypt in 1963, belonging to both the public and private sectors, see Mahfouz 1995:128.

53 These figures are taken from Okasha, "al-Qita' al-'amm," 5. Some might argue that the increase in salaries in 1963 is due to the fact that in that year, the CSI was incorporated into the GEICRT. Unlike the CSI, not only did the GEICRT get involved in cinema affairs, but it also oversaw the operation of two other means of mass communication; hence, the number of employees naturally increased. This argument, while it might explain the increase between 1962 and 1963, fails to clarify the massive increase in the total salaries of 1964.

and stagnation—only to get caught up in the labyrinth of another, namely, liquidity deficit.[54]

The hurried fashion in which these four companies were created left little if any room for advance planning or enough time for the GEICRT to raise sufficient capital,[55] hampering its future operations by undercapitalization, which was in fact the case for the entire public sector.[56] The GEICRT's budget for 1963 was spent on refurbishing and developing the film infrastructure, leaving little or no money for actual film production.[57]

Because the GEICRT was systematically trying to update the necessary tools for production, it bought the above-mentioned studios without any asset valuation, unknowingly paying much more than they should have for what were basically dead or useless assets—either not functioning properly or in desperate need of upgrading.[58] This, of course, added to the GEICRT's financial burden, for it felt obligated to renovate and equip these studios, along with the exhibition houses, with up-to-date machines before initiating film production. It comes, therefore, as no surprise that by the end of 1963, Filmontage, in spite of the number of scripts it paid advances for, had only produced three feature films, two of which had basically the same plot: Mahmud Dhulfiqar's *The Soft Hands* (*al-Aydi al-na'ima*, starring Sabah and Ahmad Mazhar), Muhammad Salim's musical film *Cairo at Night* (*al-Qahira fi-l-layl*, starring Sabah, Shadya, and Fayza Ahmad), and the remake of the latter, *Utmost Joy* (*Muntaha al-farah*, featuring Sabah, Shadya, Muhammad 'Abd al-Wahab, Farid al-Atrash, Nagwa Fuad, and Fayza Ahmad as themselves). Interestingly, the heading, "[Filmontage] presents the greatest cinematic event," was boldly positioned at the top

---

54 Ibrahim 'Umar, "Azmat al-sinima 1," *al-Ahram* 21028, 23 November 1971, 7; Naguib Mahfouz's testimony as cited in "al-Nas al-kamil li taqrir al-niyaba," 80–81.

55 Of the required capital of LE 3,570,000, only LE 2,018,000 was secured by the Ministry of Treasury. Okasha 2000:757.

56 Okasha 2000:757; see also Mursi, "al-Qita' al-'amm wa-l-istithmar al-khas," 17.

57 See the testimony of Hasan Fa'iq 'Abd al-Hamid, then general director of Bank Misr and a member of the financial committee that evaluated the public sector, in "al-Nas al-kamil li taqrir al-niyaba," 79.

58 Okasha 2000:757. For more on the issue of asset valuation, especially the case of Studio Galal, see the testimonies of Fahmi 'Ali Hasan, 'Abd al-Raziq Hasan, and Mary Butrus Yunis (Quiny) in "al-Nas al-kamil li taqrir al-niyaba," 78, 83, 85.

of *Utmost Joy*'s poster, referring probably to the wide selection of big names in hopes of attracting large numbers of moviegoers. Indeed, the reception of these films helped the GEICRT to identify weaknesses in its initial program.[59] For instance, *The Soft Hands* remained in theaters for seven consecutive weeks, outlasting all other films in 1963; paradoxically, however, its box-office revenues did not exceed LE 11,000, a very low turnover.[60] Taking into consideration that an average film's budget in the mid 1960s is roughly estimated at LE 25,000, it is reasonable to speculate that *The Soft Hands* was not commercially successful,[61] most probably for reasons that have to do with the number and kind of theaters in which it was projected. It did not escape the GEICRT's attention that this required, first, a reevaluation of its existing distribution plan, and then immediate action to increase the number of its movie theaters. In order to increase its films' revenues, the GEICRT had to improve its distribution sector, expand its exhibition capacity, and split its production division into two separate entities: one in charge of making low-budget, profit-making films to be sold to the television sector (known as B-Films) and the other responsible for the production of good quality films (A-Films). This *modus operandi* suggests the prevalence of a pragmatic approach to solving problems, based on a trial-and-error method of learning, as also appeared to be the case for other sectors of the Egyptian economy.

It is not possible, in this manuscript, to list all of the GEICRT's efforts to further expand the parameters of the public sector; only the most important ones will be analyzed. In 1963, the GEICRT sponsored the formation of the Scriptwriting Institute (Ma'had al-sinaryu), hiring respected writers and scriptwriters such Yusuf Idris, Anis Mansur, James Hetz, 'Ali al-Zurqani, Hilmi Halim, and Salah 'Izz al-Din to lecture and train students to become professional scriptwriters. This arrangement came as a reaction to the shortage of scriptwriters, a large number of whom had left Egypt (Qalyubi 1995:100). Furthermore, in mid

---

59 See the testimonies of Hasan Fa'iq 'Abd al-Hamid, Khalil Shawqi, and Yusuf Salah al-Din in "al-Nas al-kamil li taqrir al-niyaba," 79, 82.

60 The box-office revenues of *The Soft Hands* and the other films of that season were reported in *Rose al-Yusuf* no. 1884, 20 July 1964, 65.

61 As reported in *Rose al-Yusuf* based on the proceedings of a meeting held between Salah 'Amr and Egyptian filmmakers, no. 1938, 2 August 1965, 46–47. For example, the budget of an average film in 1952 was around LE 22,700. See *al-Kawakib* 76 (1952).

1964, the General Company for Distribution and Exhibition resumed relations with international distribution companies, especially after the GEICRT took over three of the most prestigious film companies in Egypt, the Eastern Company for the Cinema (al-Sharika al-sharqiya li-l-sinima),[62] Dollar Film, and the Orient Company (Sharikat al-Sharq).[63] This resulted, first, in the partial eradication of the control that some private distributors exerted over Egyptian cineastes, and second, the importation of a considerable number of foreign films which were to be screened at a number of newly built or renovated state-owned exhibition houses.[64] Additionally, cinematic delegations were sent to Baghdad, Beirut, and Rabat, among other cities, in an effort to reopen Arab markets for Egyptian film.[65] Coprofilm, under the direction of cineaste Fathi Ibrahim, also invigorated international film co-productions in Egypt by initiating its first co-productions with Italy and France, while negotiating with Algeria, Greece, India, Jordan, Kuwait, and Lebanon for potential collaboration.[66]

From 1964 onward, the GEICRT persevered in its mission to upgrade and modernize the infrastructure of the film industry. A new public production company was created by the GEICRT under the name of the Cairo Company for the Cinema (Sharikat al-Qahira li-l-sinima) to produce committed or directed films (*aflam hadifa*). A few months later, the General Company for Film Distribution and Exhibition was split into two companies, the General Company for Film Exhibition (al-Sharika al-amma li dur al-'ard) and the General Company for Film Distribution (al-Sharika al-amma li tawzi' al-aflam), increasing the number of the GEICRT's film companies from four to six. By early 1965, the recently created General Company for Film Exhibition had purchased the entire set of first-run exhibition houses

---

62 Decree no. 285 for 1964 concerning the sequestration of al-Sharika al-sharqiya li-l-sinima wa Dar sinima Rivoli, *al-Garida al-rasmiya al-misriya* 10, 13 June 1964, 74.
63 Nasir Husayn in "Limadha umimat sharikat al-tawzi'," *Rose al-Yusuf* no. 1869, 6 April 1964.
64 *Rose al-Yusuf* no. 1867, 30 March 1964, 51.
65 *Rose al-Yusuf* no. 1873, 4 May 1964, 44; no. 1885, 27 July 1964, 59; no. 1904, 7 December 1964, 42.
66 For a list of these co-productions see al-Gamal 2009. Also see *Rose al-Yusuf* no. 1896, 12 October 1964, 44; no. 1903, 30 November 1964, 42; no. 1932, 12 June 1965, 43; no. 1935, 12 July 1965, 67.

Conclusion

in Cairo from the Sequestration Committee.[67] With a view to improving the quality of film scripts, a writing bureau was established by the GEICRT, to be run by two respected writers, Sa'd Makawi and 'Abd al-Rahman al-Sharqawi, for the purpose of evaluating scripts before purchasing them.[68] In a campaign targeting the long-established star system, while also paving the path for new aspiring scriptwriters, the GEICRT's production companies were prohibited from buying the copyright of more than one novel annually from anyone, regardless of who and how famous they were. Also, filmmakers and scriptwriters were restricted to no more than three public-sector films per year.[69] This series of developments peaked in 1966, and by taking certain measures, such as bestowing on Coprofilm the exclusive right to import and distribute foreign films in Egypt,[70] the GEICRT was moving forward with its plans to rescue Egyptian cinema.

Conclusion

The wide variety of responsibilities that the GEICRT undertook shortly after its establishment, and, most importantly, the trial-and-error manner in which it pursued some of its tasks, might conceivably be construed more as an immediate response to pressing concerns than as a well-studied plan to eliminate the growing problems of the film industry. The state's initial mission was to tackle the issues of unemployment and cash-flow deficiency, both of which were successfully resolved. In so doing, the state single-handedly revived a threatened industry, but inevitably generated unexpected problems, to be discussed in the following chapter. Among the relatively large number of films (57) produced by Filmontage and the Cairo Company for the Cinema between 1963 and 1966, only a handful were critically acclaimed or commercially successful,[71] an understandable result of the hasty but prompt action plan. As for the content of some of these films, it was

---

67 *Rose al-Yusuf* no. 1894, 28 September 1964, 39.
68 The center had two departments: one for dialogue, run by Sa'd Makawi, and another for scenario, managed by 'Abd al-Rahman al-Sharqawi. *Rose al-Yusuf* no. 1934, 5 July 1965, 49.
69 *Rose al-Yusuf* no. 1912, 1 February 1965, 44.
70 *Rose al-Yusuf* no. 1963, 24 January 1966, 47.
71 See the appendix for a list of films produced by the public sector.

clear that social realist features started to appear, addressing such issues as poverty, labor, corruption, and social injustice[72]—problems that the Nasserist regime was vowing to tackle as well. Not surprisingly, the total amount of income that the public-sector films generated was insufficient for the financing of other films, leading the GEICRT to consume capital reserves, secure state subsidies, and undergo further reorganizations, all now conceivable because it was, after all, a kind of state adventure.

---

72 Among these films were Tawfiq Salih's *The Rebels* (*al-Mutamaridun*, 1968), Henri Barakat's *The Sin* (*al-Haram*, 1965), and Salah Abu Sayf's *Cairo 30* (*al-Qahira 30*, 1966).

CHAPTER 4

The End of the Public Sector in Egyptian Cinema, 1966–1971

Through steady and effective endeavors, the GEICRT achieved its primary purpose for existence—the revival of a failing national film industry. Since its inception in 1963, the GEICRT had begun to expand its parameters to include an increasing volume of film assets in a palpable effort to eliminate film stagnation and, as a by-product, reduce overall unemployment in the country. This expansion was discussed in the previous chapter, which also demonstrated how, between 1963 and 1966, the GEICRT responded quickly to mounting and usually unexpected problems. Because such challenging issues, both old and recent, required immediate action, the GEICRT's modes of operation were understandably pragmatic, making it more difficult and impractical to follow a set plan of action; hence, the drift toward an ever-changing but reactive film policy. From initially aspiring to maximize revenues in order to contribute to national economic welfare, to eventually securing loans to sustain its existence, the GEICRT's priorities revealed greater ambitions. Its ultimate objective, however, remained unaltered: to rescue an industry in jeopardy, a mission that the GEICRT single-handedly and consciously undertook.

While fairly efficient at grappling with impediments that required prompt attention, the GEICRT did not embark on tackling systemic problems. Instead it had to attend to a host of cinema-related difficulties. This is where this chapter begins. The following sections address the downsizing policy adopted by the state in 1966 to counter difficulties in the management of the cinema sector, only to have it modified in the wake of the defeat in 1967. For the first and probably last time, ideological considerations were given higher priority than economic imperatives in state film policy, manifested in a noticeable change in the political discourse of both Egyptian cinema and the public media at large. The outcome of this transformation was the ascendancy of a short-lived, politically critical national cinema. With the launching of Anwar al-Sadat's Corrective Movement (al-Haraka al-tashihiya) in 1971, which basically aimed at dismantling the Nasserist experiment including the public sector in general, both this chapter and the story of public-sector film production reach an end.

A Struggling GEICRT: Between Inherent Problems, External Problems, and Unexpected Complications

Internal Problems. Among the problems that the GEICRT inherited from the past and which dramatically affected present operations, one specific issue stands out as the most crucial and menacing of all, namely the prevalence of a profit-oriented mentality in the film industry.[1] In order to comprehend the actual threat posed by this mindset to the progress of the public sector in Egyptian cinema, we must look back to its origins and subsequent evolution. Since its beginning in the twentieth century, the film industry had been, and probably still is, commercial in orientation, concentrating exclusively on the apparent entertainment needs of the film-going public, composed overwhelmingly of the laboring and middle classes seeking consolation in the make-belief world of films.[2] In his book *The Cinema*, first published in 1936, the Egyptian director Ahmad Badrakhan, who later became chief consultant of GEICRT in 1963, explained what he regarded as the essence of Egyptian popular cinema, clearly romantic in nature:

Love is the basis of all scripts . . . . Love in cinema is simpler than in novels and plays: no psychological analysis, no conflict of conscience,

---

1 For a fuller appreciation of the inherent problems of Egyptian cinema, see 'Abd al-'Aziz 1975:140–142.
2 According to Lizbeth Malkmus, "one should know that Egyptian cinema has always been plot-oriented—if nothing else, you always get a story. This is sometimes known, pejoratively, as 'commercial' cinema." Malkmus 1988:33. For a fuller appreciation of the origins of commercial cinema, see Armbrust 1995.

none of this. All that is required is a rivalry between two men who love the same woman, or two women who vie for the love of one man, and this is what a film can best show.... A good story takes place in a location with beautiful scenery or in splendid houses, and entails the emergence of sudden or natural obstacles that threaten the protagonists' happiness and endanger their lives. However, it is much better if they are able to overcome [these difficulties] in the end.[3]

According to the film critic Samir Farid, this book was regarded as the constitution of Egyptian cinema (Farid 1995:105), introducing a formula, heavily influenced by Hollywood, that producers, filmmakers, scriptwriters, and distributors consistently followed in order to guarantee commercial success. Films challenging this formula, for example Kamil al-Tilimsani's *The Black Market* (*al-Suq al-sawda'*, 1945), though critically acclaimed, were, not surprisingly, box-office failures. A possible reason for this, if Badrakhan's explanation is taken into account, lies in the fact that the viewing public "does not like to see the world in which it lives. On the contrary, [it] aspires to see a [magic] world that can only be found in fiction" (Farid 1995:105).

Added to that equation is the dominance of private capital in the film industry. The essential tools and necessary resources for film production were predominantly in the hands of foreigners and local entrepreneurs who were largely seeking to maximize profit. This being the case, it is only logical that naive comedies, romantic melodramas, and musicals brimming with belly dancers, all of which resulted in a high turnover, prevailed on the big screen. Notwithstanding efforts made by Tal'at Harb, the founder of Bank Misr, to foster the birth of a national cinema by establishing Studio Misr and the Misr Company for Performance Arts and the Cinema, the film industry remained at the mercy of foreign investors. Paradoxically, this was regarded as the Egyptian cinema's first Golden Age, occurring "at least financially, when movie-going became the most popular form of urban entertainment in Egypt and much of the rest of the region" (Flibbert 2005:451) and

---

3 Although I was not able to find a copy of *The Cinema*, many excerpts are cited in Farid 1995:105 and Farid, "Nahwa manhag 'ilmi li kitabat tarikhuna al-sinima'i," *al-Tali'a* 3 (1973):152.

eventually making Cairo "Hollywood on the Nile."[4] Protracted exposure to this type of commercial cinema, imported or locally produced, gradually shaped the mentality of both Egyptian filmmakers and spectators to perceive films primarily as a form of entertainment and, more probably, escapism.[5]

Even after the Free Officers' Revolution succeeded in abolishing the constitutional monarchy of King Faruq and ending the British occupation of Egypt in 1952, Egyptian cinema was not transformed into a kind of revolutionary cinema, one that recognized "the most gigantic cultural, scientific, and artistic manifestation of our time, . . . the decolonization of culture."[6] Nor did the Egyptian cineastes follow in the footsteps of their Indian counterparts, who, at roughly the same time India won its independence in 1947, launched the Parallel Cinema as an alternative to the mainstream dance-and-song commercial Hindi cinema (known today as Bollywood).[7] It appears as if the received commercial conventions of filmmaking were so deeply rooted in the minds of Egyptians that neither the cineastes nor the viewing public were eager to break away from the long-established system or experience a new brand of cinematic language.[8] When the post-revolutionary regime replaced the censorship law of 1947 with a more general and

---

4 Viola Shafik, "Egyptian Cinema: Hollywood on the Nile," in *Oxford Islamic Studies Online*, http://www.oxfordislamicstudies.com/print/opr/t343/e0209 (accessed 9 April 2017). Other appellations given to the Egyptian cinema included "Hollywood of the Middle East," "Hollywood of the Arab East," and "Hollywood of the Arab World."

5 In his memoirs, Okasha explains how years of exposure to imported American films had a huge impact on the Egyptian audience's taste. Okasha 2000:777–778.

6 Also referred to as Third Cinema. The definition of Third Cinema differs from one scholar to another, but they almost unanimously agree that it is not the same as Third World Cinema, which mostly denotes "[the production] of commercial cinema that competes, with varying degrees of success, with Hollywood product in domestic markets." See Crofts 1993:54. For a fuller appreciation of the different types of cinemas, see Stam 2000; Solanas and Getino 1997:37.

7 To read more about India's Parallel Cinema, a new cinematic movement and a precursor to the Indian New Wave, see Krishen 1991:25–41.

8 Ilham Sayf al-Nasr, "George Sadoul yaktub 'an al-sinima al-misriya," *Rose al-Yusuf* no. 1927, 17 May 1965, 56–57; al-Tilimsani 1995:70. In Malkmus' words, "years of confused distribution and marketing policies in Egypt have privileged exploitation films, and filmgoers have become so used to slick, fast-paced action in movies . . . that they no longer know there is an alternative." Malkmus 1988:30.

less restrictive one in 1955,[9] many filmmakers continued to consciously, or maybe unconsciously, avoid topics or scenes that were previously prohibited by law—as is clearly evident in the films of that period.[10] The fact that these cineastes were subjected to 50 years of a politically detached and privately funded type of cinema could perhaps be viewed as the origin of this particular practice of self-censorship.[11]

However, the apparent lack of commitment on the part of Egyptian film professionals, in the sense that they did not wholeheartedly commit themselves to the mission of the revolution in decrying all forms of imperialism, should not be simply overlooked when critically analyzing Egyptian cinema.[12] It is not possible for a state to create, on its own, a cinematic movement that reflects social and political developments without the cineastes' approbation.[13] As long as Egyptian cineastes were held hostage to private capital and placed at the mercy of businessmen, they were incapable of thoroughly rejecting the capitalist system or openly challenging ingrained conventions. Fearing the shortage of funds—or worse, the disdain of viewers—filmmakers willingly continued to apply Badrakhan's formula for commercial success, replacing traditional melodramas with "revolutionary melodramas."[14] Thus, in the first years that followed the revolution, Egyptian cinema remained true to its original non-committal, profit-seeking nature.

Beginning, however, with the establishment of the public sector in Egyptian cinema in 1957, represented first by the CSI and then by the

---

9 For more details about these laws, see chapter 2, note 12.
10 For a list and analysis of some of these films, see Shafik 2007b.
11 Mustafa Darwish, "Sinima muftara 'alayha," *al-Hilal* 95 (1987); Sharaffudin 2002:82–84; Amin 2002:130. Amin speaks mainly about journalists, but his definition of self-censorship could be applied here as well.
12 The principles of the revolution were laid out in Nasser's book, *Egypt's Liberation: The Philosophy of the Revolution* (Nasser 1955).
13 Ala' al-Dib addressed a similar concern in "al-Fann wa-l-dawla," *Rose al-Yusuf* no. 1803, 31 December 1962, 44.
14 For a comprehensive survey and analysis of this type of cinema, see Gordon 2002. In another article, Gordon argues, "I do not suggest that from a cinematic perspective these films are in any way revolutionary, or that they were intended to fuel either an artistic or cultural revolution. They look and sound entirely conventional by Egyptian studio—or even Hollywood—standards. Yet by openly challenging traditional politics and social constructs, and by expressing hopes for a new Egypt, the producers of these films hoped to move the nation in bold new directions." Gordon 2001:389–390.

GEICRT from 1963 onward, attempts were made to encourage the production of quality films that adhered to a certain political and aesthetic program. Clearly, the economic, cultural, and ideological benefits of having a vigorous cinema sector had begun to be recognized by the state, propelling the creation of sustainable public film institutions. As a result of a brief cinematic awakening in the late 1950s, as mentioned in chapter two, the minister of culture and national guidance, Tharwat Okasha, founded the Higher Institute for the Cinema ultimately to serve as an incubator for next-generation film professionals, who were meant to be "responsible for the relative homogeneity and continuity of Egyptian filmmaking" (Shafik 2007a:24). Irrespective of these initiatives, the public sector was not able to liberate the film industry from the entrenched, traditional, profit-conscious mindset. Indeed, apart from a few individual endeavors reflecting a drift toward a more realistic cinematic representation of Egyptian society,[15] the models of production, distribution, and exhibition never ceased to follow those of mainstream Hollywood cinema, depending heavily on the existence of a star system and the re-projection of stale plots (Malkmus 1988:31).

External problems. The situation became more complex, and seemingly more dangerous, as the commercial mentality started to feed upon external problems, and vice versa. The administration of the public sector set out to improve the quality of films by securing loans for serious films that were deemed artistically promising or that could steer the audience in the socialist direction. The countervailing response to this development, however, came from a group of external distributors who created an alternative distribution society in Beirut, the General Organization for Distributors (al-Gam'iya al-'amma li-l-muwazi'in) in 1963, which sought to finance Egyptian private film professionals with the intention of sustaining a type of shallow cinema not that different from those produced under the old regime.[16] Furthermore, although the GEICRT had tried tirelessly to resume the exportation of Egyptian films to Arab markets, not all of the Arab governments

---

15 Examples are in chapter 2.
16 Nasir Husayn, "al-Muntig al-gadid wa ashya' ukhra," *Rose al-Yusuf* no. 1850, 25 November 1963, 44. See also Naguib Mahfouz's testimony in "al-Nas al-kamil li taqrir al-niyaba," 80.

A Struggling GEICRT

were cooperative. The establishment of the GEICRT coincided on one hand with the creation of similar institutions in Iraq, Syria, Algeria, and Tunisia,[17] and on the other hand with the rise of other national cinemas in neighboring and friendly markets such as Iran and Turkey (Poudeh and Shirvani 2008:324; Gürata 2004).The governments of these countries, now promoting and expanding their own national film production, decreased their intake of foreign films, including Egyptian films (Qalyubi 1980:61–62). If statistics are to be believed, Egypt did not export any films to Tunisia, Algeria, or Morocco in 1965, while the number of its exports to Syria dropped from 54 in 1961 to 19 in 1965, from 74 to 53 in Lebanon, 99 to 24 in Gaza, 58 to 32 in Jordan, 127 to 67 in Libya, and 69 to 25 in Sudan (Dajani 1980:94). To translate these numbers into words, this drop in the number of exported films, which historically had amounted to 60 percent of the total revenue of Egyptian film production, might plausibly explain the financial failure of some public-sector initiatives—a factor that, surprisingly, is not taken into consideration in the existing literature.

New complications. Combined, this inherited mindset and external problems were ample to stir up a crisis in the film industry, but with the addition of new complications arising from recently adopted measures, the situation inevitably exploded. When 'Abd al-Qadir Hatim succeeded Okasha in late 1962 as the minister of culture and national guidance, their different understandings of the cinema became evident, particularly their dissimilar attitudes to the film industry. Whereas Okasha regarded the cinema as a great art form conveying a cultural and educational message,[18] Hatim, who prioritized radio and television over cinema, still perceived the latter as a mere communication

---

17 In 1959, shortly after King Faysal II's government was overthrown, the new Iraqi government established the General Institution for the Cinema and Theater (al-Mu'assasa al-'amma li-l-sinima wa-l-masrah). Four years later, in 1963, its Syrian counterpart founded the Cinema Institution (Mu'assassat al-sinima). In the Maghreb the Algerian government established the National Office for Film Trade and Industry (al-Diwan al-watani li-l-tiggara wa-l-sina'a al-sinima'iya) in 1964 directly after nationalizing the film industry. That same year, the Tunisian state created the Tunisian Corporation for Film Production and Expansion (Société Anonyme Tunisienne de Production et d'Expansion Cinématographique—SATPAC).

18 To learn more about Okasha's perception of the cinema, see his speech at the National Assembly on 16 June 1969 as cited in Wahba 1972:34–35.

instrument, reliant for its success on the production of films tailored to the presumed tastes of the Egyptian public.[19] Apart from this, the sociopolitical and economic transformations that Egypt was experiencing at the time Hatim was appointed drove him to take more drastic and interventionist actions than his predecessor. Shortly after the creation of the GEICRT, Hatim began actual public film production, which in fact ignited a debilitating eight-year competition between an anxious private sector and an ambitious public sector.[20] Allegedly, the public sector was supposed to produce high-quality and engaged films that the private sector, with so much at stake, was not willing to finance,[21] assuming that the former was now free from the financial constraints and commercial stipulations insisted upon by private film distributors.[22] However, this did not really happen, as shown in the preceding section. Instead of commissioning the production of a limited number of quality films that aimed at generalizing the new socialist principles of the National Charter, the GEICRT, for various considerations discussed in the previous chapter, was obliged to produce a large number of low-budget films.

Moreover, among the public sector's many responsibilities was providing technical services and financial assistance to the private sector as well, which remained subject to the old profit-seeking mentality. Thus the cinema as an industry was saved, but not yet liberated from the flaws of the past. Between 1963 and 1966, the GEICRT produced

---

19 For more details about this conflict between qualitative and quantitative film policies, see Abu Shadi 2000b:321 and Gordon 2002:31. On the growing tension between the cultural and informational aspects of the GEICRT, see al-Gamal 2009:35. Also see the testimonies of Naguib Mahfouz and Muhammad Raga'i in "al-Nas al-kamil li taqrir al-niyaba," 80, 84.

20 According to Ihsan 'Abd al-Qudus, the competition between the private and public sectors did not stand on a healthy basis; a yearly plan supervised the cooperation and coordination between them. *Rose al-Yusuf* no. 1864, 2 March 1964, 42.

21 In Magdi Wahba's words, the public sector was to "sponsor a young generation of filmmakers, especially the graduates of the Higher Institute [for the] Cinema, for films which might not find a ready response among the more commercially minded producers of the private sector." Wahba 1972:33.

22 To name one of these constraints, external film distributors preferred to finance films that featured well-known actors in hopes of garnering commercial success, thus sustaining a long-established star system. Nasir Husayn, "Harb al-a'sab dud al-sinima al-misriya," *Rose al-Yusuf* no. 2021, 6 March 1967, 34.

57 public films and funded an additional 37 private films,[23] of which only six were deemed artistically valuable by film critics, while the rest were unoriginal replicas of the pre–public sector conventional cinema or which copied American films.[24]

Furthermore, in the absence of any sense of collective commitment on the part of the cineastes, incidents of squandered public funds started to surface. Now that advances and funds were secured by the public sector, some cineastes, including actors, directors, and technicians, availed themselves of this opportunity to fill their pockets. The budget of an average public film greatly exceeded that of a private one for no apparent reason. The salaries of film professionals contracted by the public sector doubled, or even tripled, as did the amount of film stock used in the production of a public film. The shooting schedules of public films were extended deliberately, more often than not.[25] When the Ministry of Culture and National Guidance decided in 1964 to replace monetary prizes, given away during film festivals or as incentives granted to artists working in the film industry, with symbolic awards in an effort to reduce expenditures, the cineastes, as was reported in the press, condemned the decision and openly opposed it.[26] This could perhaps be viewed as an indication of the preoccupation of a number of cineastes with financial concerns rather than the quality of the films they were supposed to furnish.[27] When the chairman of the GEICRT, Salah 'Amr,

---

23 In an interview with Su'ad Zuhayr, Yusuf Salah al-Din, the general director of the General Company for Distribution, claimed that the number of private films funded by the GEICRT between 1963 and 1965 was 37, costing around LE 850,000. *Rose al-Yusuf* no. 1969, 7 March 1966, 43–45.

24 The critically acclaimed public films that were produced between 1963 and 1966 were 'Abd al-Rahman al-Khamisi's *The Penalty* (*al-Gaza'* [1965], starring Shams al-Barudi and Husayn al-Sharbini); Khalil Shawqi's *The Mountain* (*al-Gabal* [1965], starring Salah Qabil and Samira Ahmad); Henri Barakat's *The Sin* (*al-Haram* [1965], starring Fatin Hamama and 'Abdullah al-Ghayth); Husayn Kamal's *The Impossible* (*al-Mustahil* [1965], starring Salah Mansur and Fathiya Shahin); Salah Abu Sayf's *Cairo 30* (*al-Qahira 30* [1966], starring Hamdi Ahmad, Su'ad Husni, and Ahmad Mazhar); and Fatin 'Abd al-Wahab's *My Wife, A General Director* (*Merati mudir 'amm* [1966], starring Shadya and Salah Dhulfiqar).

25 For more details about these incidents, see *Rose al-Yusuf* no. 1888, 17 August 1964, 44; no. 1969, 7 March 1966, 43–45; no. 2017, 6 February 1967, 16–17.

26 As reported by Gamil al-Baguri in *Rose al-Yusuf* no. 1878, 23 March 1964, 44–45.

27 Hasan 1995:224–225; Nasir Husayn, "Mahraganat li-shira' al-kravatat," *Rose al-Yusuf* no. 1871, 20 April 1964.

invited filmmakers commissioned by the public sector to his office to openly discuss the production plan of 1965–1966 in terms of content, quantity, and quality, only 12 of them attended.[28] This nonchalance that some cineastes exhibited about their presumed role in the intended cultural revolution that Nasser called for, and which he viewed as a natural by-product of his political and social revolution,[29] is echoed in Rushdi Abaza's explanation of the actors' need for higher salaries:

> *I have two cars, one that is ordinary and another parked in front of my house for twenty-eight days a month, which I only use when I want to meet with my fans. These all cost money. Every season, I have to buy sixty suits, most of which I wear while filming. We live under extraordinary circumstances that obligate us to live in luxury. . . . I guess if I was to be chauffeured in a Rolls Royce to the Berlin [Film Festival], I would have returned [to Egypt] with the third prize. Cinema is [about] slyness and appearances and we Egyptians are the masters of such things.*[30]

Nevertheless, Egyptian cineastes were not the only ones to blame for the severity of the situation, that is, the maintenance of this profit-prodigal mentality; bureaucrats working for the GEICRT also had a hand in aggravating it. Although very beneficial to the continuation of the Egyptian film industry, the measures taken by the GEICRT between 1963 and 1966 started to backfire before too long. To begin with, the fundamental problem had to do with the complications arising from the massive influx of employees coming from different fields to work at the GEICRT or one of its companies. That there were not enough jobs for all of these employees did not stop the Ministry of Culture and National Guidance from carrying on a wild and random recruiting process. Several newly created posts had no actual function at all—for example, the executive producer (*muntig munafidh*), who

---

28 *Rose al-Yusuf* no. 1938, 2 August 1965, 46–47.
29 Naguib Mahfouz and Sa'd al-Din Wahba addressed the lack of commitment on the part of the cineastes in their testimonies in "al-Nas al-kamil li taqrir al-niyaba," 80, 87.
30 Rushdi Abaza, proceedings of the *Arba' mu'tamarat* that were held on 12 and 13 October 1966. See also Salah Hafiz, "Hal intaha 'asr al-sinima'i al-gahil," *Rose al-Yusuf* no. 2023, 20 March 1967, 30–32.

received a monthly salary without doing any work (Murad 1991:207). Many of the hired employees, who lacked any sense of forward-looking planning, were appointed in positions that they knew very little about, resulting in the purchase of plots and stories that were not adaptable to the big screen.[31] In principle, there was no rule obligating anyone working in and for the public sector to sever ties with the private sector. However, in some cases, a producer hired by the Cairo Company for Film Production, for example, was not allowed to produce or participate in any other project funded by another company, either public or private. This condition was not fully respected. Subhi Farhat, 'Abbas Hilmi, Hilmi Rafla, Ramsis Naguib, and Mahmud Kamil are only a few of the people who, though working for the Cairo Company, continued to produce films for the private sector.[32]

This inefficient bureaucracy, though condemned repeatedly by Nasser,[33] was also an automatic aftereffect of the primitive organizational structure of the GEICRT, which generally depended upon complete functional and sectorial divisions (*al-taqsim al-naw'i*) in managing its companies.[34] Taking into consideration the fact that the Egyptian film industry had suffered from the beginning from a lack of coordination between its subsectors, this type of partition only added fuel to the fire. One reason that might explain such a shortsighted decision lies in the GEICRT's over-enthusiasm and the short timeframe within which it was operating, which required hasty intervention. Instead of adhering to a socialist model of organization—now that Egypt aspired to become a model for socialist change—it continued to abide by a somewhat

---

31 "al-Sinima al-misriya fi khatar," *al-Hilal* no. 10, 1 October 1967, 114–116; Ibrahim 'Umar, "Azmat al-sinima 1" *al-Ahram*, 23 November 1971,7. It was reported in *Rose al-Yusuf* in 1965 that the planning unit in GEICRT found, in reviewing the stories purchased by Filmontage between 1963 and 1965, that the latter bought 55 stories for which it paid between LE 400 and LE 1,000 as advances, and of which only 10 could be adapted to the big screen. No. 1917, 8 March 1965, 44. See also the testimonies of Fahmi 'Ali Hasan and 'Abd al-Raziq Hasan in "al-Nas al-kamil li taqrir al-niyaba," 83, 85.

32 'Adli Fahim, "Hikayat al-sinima," *Rose al-Yusuf* no. 2049, 18 September 1967, 22–25.

33 Nasser was aware that inefficient bureaucracy was spreading throughout the whole public sector. He addressed its impact on the country and the need to eliminate it in his speech during the opening session of the Maglis al-umma in 1965, as reported in *al-Tali'a* 10 (1965).

34 As reported by Nasir Husayn, *Rose al-Yusuf* no. 1967, 21 February 1966, 44.

archaic structure. A common socialist pattern of organizing a film sector, as it was reported by some Egyptian film critics in the press, entailed the establishment of production units, each of which contained its own studio, a distribution department, and a selected number of exhibition houses, all operating in harmony to serve film production.[35] Unlike such systems, the GEICRT's companies worked independently,[36] each one seeking to maximize its own profit, sometimes at the expense of its sister companies, which had a devastating effect on the quality of their common product, Egyptian films.[37] Under such circumstances, the business-oriented private sector, the largest beneficiary of this unhealthy competition between the public-sector companies, continued to survive and even expand. The press criticized this situation heavily, cynically observing how the Egyptian film industry had become a "big restaurant [where] the private sector eats and the public sector pays."[38]

The GEICRT Reorganized: Prevailing over Difficulties

At around the same time, articles by journalists, artists, and intellectuals such as Naguib Mahfouz, Louis 'Awad, and Gamil al-Baguri started appearing in the daily *al-Ahram*, the popular *Rose al-Yusuf*, and the leftist *al-Tali'a*, denouncing the naive and deteriorating quality of films, and at the same time calling for a more refined and engaged cinema.[39] These articles covered news about international cinemas, including but not

---

35 Nasir Husayn, *Rose al-Yusuf* no. 1967, 21 February 1966, 44.
36 These companies were Filmontage, Coprofilm, the Cairo Company, the General Company for Studios, and the General Company for Film Exhibition and Distribution. *Rose al-Yusuf* no. 1965, 7 February 1966, 40. See also Gamal al-Laythi's and Sa'd al-Din Wahba's interviews in *Rose al-Yusuf* no. 1967, 21 February 1966, 44–45.
37 In his articles, Ahmad Hamrush addresses the harmful competition between Filmontage and the Cairo Company represented by their respective chairmen, Sa'd al-Din Wahba and Gamal al-Laythi. *Rose al-Yusuf* no. 2068, 29 January 1968, 37. See also the testimonies of Samir Ahmad 'Askar, a member of a committee formed to reassess the cinema sector, 'Abd al-Raziq Hasan, and Sa'd al-Din Wahba in "al-Nas al-kamil li taqrir al-niyaba," 80, 86–87.
38 *Rose al-Yusuf* no. 2201, 17 August 1970, 36. For a few examples, see Ahmad Hamrush, *Rose al-Yusuf* no. 1967, 21 February 1966, 46; 'Umar Ibrahim, "Azmat al-sinima 2," *al-Ahram* no. 21029, 24 November 1971, 7.
39 Interview with Naguib Mahfouz, Nasir Husayn in *Rose al-Yusuf* no. 1955, 29 November 1965, 43–44; Gamil al-Baguri, *Rose al-Yusuf* no. 1875, 18 May 1964, 48; Louis 'Awad, "Khitab maftuh ila wazir al-thaqafa," *al-Ahram*, 19 November 1965.

limited to updates about socialist, revolutionary, neo-realist, and New Wave cinema.[40] In his article "Toward a Socialist Cinema," appearing in *al-Tali'a*, Salah Abu Sayf defined socialist cinema as follows:

> *The cinema of the masses [could only be achieved] if cineastes learn both the language and problems of the masses, . . . it is the cineaste's responsibility to . . . glorify the people's actions, to protect the state's national interests and public policy, to denounce . . . colonialism.*[41]

Abu Sayf's counterpart, Gamal al-Laythi, also made an effort to raise awareness among the cineastes about the necessity of having a committed socialist cinema, pointing out that "any film which serves a political, humanistic, or social cause serves our society."[42] Additionally, voices advocating the separation of culture from national guidance, and by extension, art and cinema from radio and television, started to appear.[43] Even Okasha had envisioned such a separation before his return to the ministry (Okasha 2000:713–714). Also, graduates from the Higher Institute for the Cinema and the Scriptwriting Institute, both pioneering ventures of the public sector, began operations, bringing with them a fresh, alternative perception and understanding of the cinema. In this atmosphere, the state deemed it necessary to reassess and modify its film policy, in part to address the above-mentioned cumulative predicaments, as well as to respond to this growing demand for better quality and more ideologically conscious cinema.

As a first measure, Nasser issued a decree in late 1965 separating culture from national guidance, followed shortly by two consecutive

---

40 For example, a mention of the Chinese cinema, "the true socialist cinema," appeared in *Rose al-Yusuf* no. 1962, 17 January 1966; Mufid al-Gaza'iri wrote about Czechoslovakian cinema in "Tagrubat al-qita' al-'amm fi-l-sinima al-tshikiya," *Rose al-Yusuf* no. 1964, 31 January 1966, 43–44; the renowned French filmmaker Alain Resnais was quoted in an article about the French New Wave in *Rose al-Yusuf* no. 1982, 6 June 1966, 39, and "Fi-l-sinima 'indahum mamnu' al-dala' amma 'indana??," *Rose al-Yusuf* no. 1989, 25 July 1966, 72.
41 Salah Abu Sayf, "Nahwa fann sinima'i ishtiraki," *al-Tali'a* 6 (1965): 93–96.
42 Gamal al-Laythi, *Akhir Sa'a*, 31 August 1966, 38. Also cited in Gordon 2002:205.
43 Louis 'Awad, "Kalima sadika 'an al-mawsam al-masrahi" and "Khitab maftuh ila wazir al-thaqafa," *al-Ahram*, 30 April 1965 and 19 November 1965; and *Rose al-Yusuf* no. 1948, 11 October 1965, 49.

laws in early 1966.⁴⁴ While the first ordinance aimed at reorganizing the Ministry of National Guidance, placing under its purview radio and television,⁴⁵ the second restructured the Ministry of Culture, giving more emphasis than before to the artistic aspect of the cinema. Not only did the Ministry of Culture aim to raise the professional and artistic level of film production, but it also sought to cultivate an alternative cinematic taste, introducing the Egyptian viewing public to new genres of non-commercial cinema. Furthermore, in an effort to supervise and maintain the artistic quality of film production, the ministry established the General Directory for Artistic Censorship (al-Idara al-'amma li-l-raqaba 'ala al-musanifat al-fanniya) to examine stories and films before purchasing and screening them respectively.⁴⁶ As for the ministry's administration, Nasser appointed Sulayman Huzayyin as the interim minister. Under the latter's supervision, the Secretariat of Propaganda and Thought (Amanat al-da'wa wa-l-fikr) of the Socialist Union convened a meeting with the cineastes to address their complaints and suggestions.⁴⁷ Attesting to its responsiveness, the state decreed a new law, thoroughly reorganizing the GEICRT. It became known as the General Egyptian Institution for the Cinema (al-Mu'assassa al-misriya al-'amma li-l-sinima—hereafter GEIC).⁴⁸

For almost a year, the GEIC remained leaderless as several potential candidates declined to chair an underfunded institution.⁴⁹ In the meantime, Nasser had succeeded in convincing Okasha to accept his nomination to become the minister of culture, giving him the urgent mission of "containing the [artistic and financial] damage suffered by the cinema sector" (Okasha 2000:712). Because Nasser was aware that the state could not afford to waste funds on faltering projects, he instructed Okasha, as the latter recounted, to temporarily halt production for a two-year period, in order to focus on systemically addressing

---

44 *Rose al-Yusuf* no. 1948, 11 October 1965, 49; no. 1952, 8 November 1965, 45.
45 Presidential Decree no. 76 for 1966, *al-Garida al-rasmiya al-misriya* 16, 18 January 1966, 61–62.
46 Presidential Decree no. 449 for 1966, *al-Garida al-rasmiya al-misriya* 39, 17 February 1966, 164–165.
47 *Rose al-Yusuf* no. 1965, 7 February 1966, 39.
48 Presidential Decree no. 453 for 1966, *al-Garida al-rasmiya al-misriya* 42, 21 February 1966, 181–182.
49 As reported by *Rose al-Yusuf* no. 1954, 22 November 1965, 44.

difficulties within the film industry (Okasha 2000:713–714, 778). Mindful of the shortcomings of previous film policies, mainly the lack of advance planning, Okasha's first cautious measure was to launch a series of investigations. To achieve this, he formed a committee of economists from the Central Auditing Agency (al-Gihaz al-markazi li-l-muhasabat) to inspect the financial state of the institution and suggest possible solutions (Okasha 2000:755). To review the technical and artistic standing of the GEIC and its assets, he hired a group of French experts, among whom was the renowned screenwriter Pierre Cardinale, with the intention of uncovering the real reasons behind the deterioration of Egyptian films.[50] Okasha, however, was sensible enough to realize that introducing any external solution prior to consultation with the local cinematic circle would not be well received by them. For this reason he summoned a cinema conference on 12 and 13 October 1966, in which a large number of film professionals participated.[51] A closer examination of the interventions proposed at the conference reveals a deep schism in the cineastes' perception of both the cinema and the presumed role of the public sector. On the one hand, there was a group of professionals who expressed a sense of responsibility and commitment to a socialist cinema, while on the other hand, another group typified the traditional commercial mindset, opposing a politically and socially committed cinema.[52]

The proceedings of this conference, the reports of the two aforementioned investigative committees, and a number of articles published at the time also identified difficulties that were obstructing the GEIC's development,[53] predictably suggesting a similar set of resolutions, among which was the recommendation for a complete change in the structure of the public companies before the introduction of any other

---

50 Hafiz, "Hal intaha 'asr al-sinima'i," 30–32; Okasha 2000:757–760; Okasha, "al-Qita' al-'amm," 3.

51 The cinema conference was part of a broader one, addressing the problems of four different sectors: the cinema, the theater, books, and fine arts. For its proceedings, see *Arba' mu'tamarat*.

52 Hashim al-Nahas, "al-Ganib al-akhar fi mu'tamar al-sinima'iyyin . . . laysat hambaka wa lakinaha fann wa risala," *al-Kawakib*, 25 October 1966, 30–33.

53 For an example of articles addressing this crisis, see Salah Abu Sayf, "Mustaqbal al-film al-'arabi wa-l-mustawa al-fanni . . . wa-l-tadhawuq al-gamahiri," *al-Tali'a* 8 (1966): 99–103.

measure.⁵⁴ The sectorial fragmentation of the public companies, the lack of advance planning, the employment of unqualified personnel, the shortage of qualified employees, the implications of the sociopolitical transformations that Egypt was witnessing in general, and the commercially minded private sector were found to be the real triggers for the artistic and financial crisis of the cinema sector. Okasha's straightforward response was, "I cannot do miracles but I will do my utmost to [incorporate these suggestions]."⁵⁵ For a while, at least, this promise reignited the cineastes' hopes for a more effective GEIC. Okasha kept his word. Two months after the conference, on 20 December 1966, Decree 48 was issued, restructuring the GEIC by merging its six companies into two entities: the Cairo Company for Film Production (Sharikat al-Qahira li-l-sinima), under the supervision of the economist 'Abd al-Raziq Hasan, and the Cairo Company for Film Distribution and Exhibition (Sharikat al-Qahira li dur al-'ard wa-l-tawzi'), operating under the financial expert Yusuf Salah al-Din (Okasha 2000:761). Okasha's decision to appoint economic specialists as general directors of public film companies falls in line with Nasser's directions to protect the film public sector from further financial loss. Nevertheless, the artistic level of Egyptian cinema was still at the front of Okasha's mind, as was manifested, first, by the appointment of Naguib Mahfouz, probably one of Egypt's most influential literary figures at the time, as the president of the GEIC, as well as the allocation of one-third of the ministry's entire budget to the GEIC (Okasha 2000:761; see also Wahba 1972:32).

The three appointees instantly introduced what was referred to as the 'downsizing policy' (*siyasat al-inkimash*) by contrast to the overambitious policy of the preceding administration—carefully examining stories prior to their purchase, diligently following up on previous productions begun before their tenures, and, most importantly, cutting the wages of employees and film professionals as well as reducing unnecessary expenses, which, of course, provoked an uproar from the cineastes.⁵⁶

---

54 For a full list of these suggestions, see al-Nahas, "al-Ganib al-akhar fi mu'tamar al-sinima'iyyin," 30–33.

55 For an excerpt of Ukasha's speech at the end of the conference, see *Arba' mu'tamarat*.

56 "al-Sinima al-misriya fi khatar," *al-Hilal* no. 10, 1 October 1967, 116–117; 'Umar, "Azmat al-sinima 1" and "Azmat al-sinima 3," respectively in *al-Ahram* nos. 21028, 23 November 1971, 7, and 21030, 25 November 1971, 7. See also 'Abd al-Raziq Hasan's testimony in "al-Nas al-kamil li taqrir al-niyaba," 85.

Not surprisingly, 80 percent of the GEIC's budget was spent on paying up previous debts and loans owed to several creditors and departments. In so doing, the GEIC's new administration became aware of possible liquidity consequences that might hamper the institution's future operations. This suggested to Okasha the necessity of finding other funding sources, if only to secure the employees' salaries and social insurances. Okasha, in turn, informed Nasser about this situation, appealing for immediate help, which the latter provided by calling upon the minister of finance to secure a new loan for the GEIC.[57]

Artistic, technical, and administrative improvements also accompanied this downsizing policy. Within a one-year period beginning in late 1966, the Ministry of Culture introduced several reforms in hopes of raising the artistic level of Egyptian cinema. In an effort to inform peasants, through films, about the new socialist experience that Egypt was undergoing, the Directory of Mass Culture (Idarat al-thaqafa al-gamahiriya) was created with Sa'd Kamil as its director, with the intention of spreading mass culture to the less privileged provinces and small villages (Mursi and Wahba 1973:71). Moreover, in an attempt to introduce unconventional film genres, the National Center for Documentary and Short Films (al-Markaz al-watani li-l-aflam al-watha'iqiya wa-l-qasira) was established as an autonomous unit within the GEIC, to be run by the artist Hasan Fuad.[58] In light of these developments, it is possible to conclude that greater emphasis was given to the quality and content of films than ever before. Interestingly, the public sector continued to support the private sector financially, but not without introducing a set of stipulations. Any producer going beyond either the fixed production schedule or the assigned amount of film stock had to personally pay the extra costs.[59] "We are not asking for much," 'Abd al-Raziq Hasan informed the cineastes, "but to produce good films that are compatible with the state's discourse"[60]—that is, the socialist direction—thus

---

57 This information was taken from two reports, one prepared by 'Abd al-Raziq Hasan and another by Naguib Mahfouz, as cited in Okasha 2000:761–762 and "al-Qita' al-'amm al-sinima'i," 17.
58 Okasha, "al-Qita' al-'amm al-sinima'i," 18; Sa'id 1994:46–47.
59 As reported by Nasir Husayn, *Rose al-Yusuf* no. 2025, 3 April 1967, 44.
60 Interview with 'Abd al-Raziq Hasan as reported by Hilmi Hilal, *Rose al-Yusuf* no. 2022, 13 March 1967, 30–31.

summarizing the GEIC's primary objective in a few words. Additionally, by commissioning Husayn Kamal, a graduate of the Higher Institute for the Cinema, to launch the GEIC's production plan for 1967, this new administration displayed a genuine interest in opening the doors to a new generation of skilled and talented filmmakers, probably with the undeclared intention of cleansing the cinematic scene of traditionally minded professionals.[61]

The least that could be said about these developments is that they reflected the government's resolve to improve the cinema sector, not only financially but artistically as well, all the while operating under difficult circumstances. Clearly, the priority given to art-related concerns marks a significant change in the cultural policy of the state, probably revealing a new, more comprehensive perception of the cinema on the part of both the cineastes and the government. As a result, some critics dubbed this period, so heavily influenced by the downsizing policy, a time of great administrative achievement.[62]

On the Heels of the Defeat

On 5 June 1967, Israel launched a series of massive airstrikes against Egyptian airfields, taking the Egyptians and the Arab world by surprise. This attack led to the outbreak of the Six-Day War between Israel on one side and Egypt, Jordan, and Syria on the other. Not only did this war inflict heavy losses on Egypt, it also resulted in open encroachment on Egyptian sovereignty, materialized in the Israeli occupation of the Sinai. "It was this defeat," according to the film critic Qussai Samak, "that brought back the national question in its most immediate aspects to the center of Egypt's preoccupations" (Samak 1979:32). A need to compensate for and respond to this military defeat by means of some sort of a cultural resistance, which denounced the enemy and exalted the nation, was evident in the state's post-1967 film policy. For the first time in the history of Egyptian cinema, ideological concerns were prioritized over economic imperatives. After the defeat, the Ministry of Culture called upon the administration of the cinema sector

---

61 Nasir Husayn, *Rose al-Yusuf* no. 2025, 3 April 1967, 44. See also Salah Abu Sayf's and 'Abd al-Raziq Hasan's testimonies in "al-Nas al-kamil li taqrir al-niyaba," 85–86.
62 Nasir Husayn, *Rose al-Yusuf* no. 2255, 30 August 1971, 36–37.

to explicitly abide by the government's new stance[63] that aimed at "a conscious mass mobilization that could prepare the masses for a long and hard struggle through a number of films, which valorize bravery, patience, sanctification of duty" (Okasha 2000:764).

Consequently, the state officially banned the importation of British and American films, both as a political statement against these states' blatant support of Israel and as a cultural rejection of the type of commercial cinema they projected.[64] To find a replacement for these films, the GEIC turned its eyes toward new "friendly" governments in hopes of importing films that revolved around the idea of "the masses [being] the true hero in national struggles."[65] Nevertheless, without providing an alternative cinema, the ban alone could not possibly end the existing politically puerile cinema. In September 1967, in an effort to encourage a more committed cinema, Okasha dispatched a delegation to several socialist countries to learn more about their cinemas, with a view to transferring their knowledge and expertise to Egypt.[66] Among the techniques learned was the "Pocket Film" (*sinima al-gayb*), which involved the use of small cameras and natural sources of light to visually document reality as it is, creating in the process short art and experimental films,[67] a concept that completely contradicted the practice of commercial cinema. Also, European and Soviet film weeks were held in Cairo and Alexandria. The *cinéma d'auteur*[68] was another type of cinema that Roberto Rossellini, the Italian neo-realist filmmaker, helped to spread among Egyptian filmmakers after accepting Okasha's invitation to host a film workshop in Egypt.[69]

---

63 This stance is explained in detail in Nasser's declaration to the nation on 30 March 1968. http://nasser.bibalex.org/Data/GR09_1/Speeches/1968/680330_bayanat.htm (accessed 11 April 2017).

64 Of course, this ban did not last for too long. See *Bulletin d'information du Centre interarabe du cinéma et de la télévision*, 22, 30 June 1967, 7.

65 Hilmi Hilal and Nasir Husayn, "Saytarat al-sharikat al-amrikiya ma zalat qa'ima," *Rose al-Yusuf* no. 2040, 17 July 1967, 28–29.

66 Nasir Husayn, *Rose al-Yusuf* no. 2050, 25 September 1967, 31–32.

67 *Rose al-Yusuf* no. 2059, 27 November 1967, 32.

68 It appeared in Hilmi Hilal's article in *Rose al-Yusuf* no. 2059, 27 November 1967, 33. The notion of *cinéma d'auteur* first appeared in France in the 1950s, influenced by the theories of Louis Delluc, Alexandre Astruc, and André Bazin; it refers to filmmakers with a distinguishable style or thematic preoccupation. To read more about it, see Demiray 2014.

69 *Rose al-Yusuf* no. 2059, 27 November 1967, 33.

This urge to take a cultural stand vis-à-vis the national crisis was not restricted to state institutions. The impact of the defeat on the Egyptians in general, and the artists in particular, worked as a wake-up call for film professionals to revolutionize and ultimately politicize their cinema. A growing demand for "a different type of cinema, a new cinematic language, a new mentality, a new vision" started spreading among the cineastes. Devastated by the defeat, the students at the Higher Institute for the Cinema used their skills and the resources provided by the institute to produce short films about civic engagement and citizenship (Murad 1991:212). This initiative caught the eye of the GEIC's administration, which clearly started conceiving of films as a political weapon, compelling the National Center for Documentary and Short Films to sponsor them.[70] In one of his speeches after the defeat, Nasser addressed his people, urging them to resist: "Now that the military aggression is over, a [cultural] attack will transpire [against] the people, [against] every citizen of this country."[71] Memorable mobilizing slogans such as "A camera in one hand and a weapon in another" started appearing in the press, ultimately recognizing cinema as a major weapon of resistance. In such an atmosphere, cinema became "the eye of truth ... which could ... record the cruelty of defeat and the glory of victory."[72]

Another response to the defeat was the launch of several publications calling for new and avant-garde cultural movements, like *Gallery 68*, a journal focusing on literature and visual arts.[73] Under the direction of Raga' al-Naqash, *al-Kawakib* dedicated an entire sector, entitled "Angry Magazine" (*al-Magalla al-ghadiba*), to the New Cinema Collective (Gama'at al-sinima al-gadida). The latter was a film society created by a group of young filmmakers, among whom were graduates of the Higher Institute for the Cinema,[74] itself the creation of the public sector.

---

70 Muhammad Khalafullah, *Rose al-Yusuf* no. 2038, 3 July 1967, 31–32.

71 *Rose al-Yusuf* no. 2042, 31 July 1967, 37.

72 *Rose al-Yusuf* no. 2036, 19 June 1967, 24.

73 Ahmad Rif'at, "On the Importance of Post-1967 Alternative Cinematic Adventures in Egypt," *al-Arabiya*, 15 September 2016, http://www.madamasr.com/en/2016/09/15/feature/culture/on-the-importance-of-post-1967-alternative-cinematic-adventures-in-egypt/ (accessed 10 March 2017).

74 Chapter two mentions the establishment of this institute in light of its significance and novelty.

'Ali Abu Shadi, Samir Farid, Ahmad Mutwali, 'Adil Munir, Muhammad Radi, Ra'fat al-Mihi, and Ashraf Fahmi were among its members.[75] Like its counterparts in Latin America and France, this society published a manifesto in which it attacked the deep-rooted commercial mentality that prevailed in Egyptian cinema, labeling it "the opiate of the Arab masses" (Samak 1979:33; Sharaffudin 2002:122). Greatly influenced by realist and revolutionary cinemas, this society called for an alternative cinema that "would record and study the movement of Egyptian society," tracking the developing social and political relations (Samak 1979:33). Finding in this society's manifesto the type of cinema that it aspired to, the GEIC collaborated with its members on two quality films. The first film was 'Ali 'Abd al-Khaliq's *A Song along the Passage* (*Ughniya 'ala al-mammar*, 1972), which addressed the trauma and struggle of Egyptian soldiers stuck in a strategic checkpoint during the Six-Day War. *Shadows on the Other Side* (*Zilal 'ala al-ganib al-akhar*, 1974), the second collaboration with the society, was directed by Ghalib Sha'th, a Palestinian filmmaker who started his career in Egypt after finishing his studies in Vienna.[76]

Together with the previous downsizing policy, these cultural transformations that Egypt experienced on the heels of the defeat facilitated the emergence of a politically critical, national cinema, marked by the artistic "improvement in the intellectual caliber of [its] films" (Gordon 2002:209). Looking back at the prevailing cinematic spirit after the defeat, director Khayri Bishara pointed out that "we wanted to change the course of [Egyptian cinema]."[77] Indeed, this period witnessed the production of some of the most influential and highly acclaimed films in the history of Egyptian cinema. In addition to visually depicting the aftermath of the Six-Day War, the makers of these films attempted to uncover what they assumed were the real reasons for the defeat, suggesting factors other than an "imperialist

---

75 al-Qalyubi 1980:70–71; Amir al-'Umari, "Ghalib Sha'th batal al-zilal wa-l-ganib al-akhar," *al-'Arab*, 11 October 2015, http://www.alarab.co.uk/pdf/2015/10/11-10/p16.pdf (accessed 12 February 2017).
76 al-'Umari, "Ghalib Sha'th."
77 An excerpt from an interview with Khayri Bishara by *Al Jazeera*, entitled "Khayri Bishara . . . al-waqi'iya al-gadida fi-l-sinima al-misriya," http://www.aljazeera.net/programs/thearabiclens/2006/9/4/خيري-بشارة-الواقعية-الجديدة-فى-السينما-المصرية

conspiracy" and "fate."[78] Some of them considered the defeat an artistic and emotional stimulus, directly addressing it, decrying it, speaking back to it, and analyzing it; others occupied themselves with allegorical criticism of the regime and the demise of its national project.[79] Not only did these films grapple with sociopolitical and existentialist issues, but also their filmic language reflected, on the one hand, a refined sense of cinematic maturity, and on the other, a recognizable change in the cinema's discourse, neither of which would have transpired without the contribution of the public sector.

The Dissolution of the GEIC

While the GEIC was embarking on a mission to revolutionize the cinema sector, its debts to the Ministry of Finance and the Industrial Bank were rising substantially. During a cabinet session in April 1968, the minister of finance announced his intention to reduce his ministry's funding to the GEIC, for the latter, he argued, had become a financial burden on the state. In reaction to this, Okasha posed the traditional rhetorical question: "Is culture a commercial commodity subject to the law of supply and demand?" Not expecting an answer, he went on to note: "It is not logical for cultural institutions to serve two masters simultaneously and with equal devotion. It is either the quality [of films] or their box-office revenues" (Okasha 2000:770–771.)

---

78 In the words of Salah Abu Sayf, "there was a defeat because many . . . exploited the people in the name of socialism while they do not have anything to do with it . . . . The question is: reform or revolution? . . . when everything is corrupt we do not need renovation . . . we need change and a radical one." In Samak 1977:15.

79 A question might be posed here: "Why did a police state allow the screening of such political films?" In their attempt to answer it, many scholars argue that "by screening such films, the state was actually being clever, expressing a high level of political shrewdness"; al-Gayyar 2000:15–23. Others designate this period "a period of 'thaw' in which government censors allowed a greater degree of more explicit political criticism of the regime"; Gordon 2002:31. To name a few examples: Youssef Chahine's *The Land* (*al-Ard*, 1970), *The Choice* (*al-Ikhtiyar*, 1971), and *The Sparrow* (*al-'Usfur*, 1972); Kamal al-Shaykh's *The Man Who Lost His Shadow* (*al-Ragul al-ladhi faqada zilahu*, 1968), *Miramar* (1969), and *Dusk and Dawn* (*Ghurub wa-shuruq*, 1970); Husayn Kamal's *A Little Bit of Fear* (*Shay' min al-khawf*, 1969); Tawfiq Salih's *Diary of a Country Prosecutor* (*Yawmiyat na'ib fi-l-aryaf*, 1969); Salah Abu Sayf's *Dawn of Islam* (*Fagr al-Islam*, 1971); Shu'ban Ibrahim's *My Wife and the Dog* (*Zawgati wa-l-kalb*, 1971); and last but definitely not least, Shadi 'Abd al-Salam's *The Mummy* (*al-Mummya'*, 1969).

One month later, in May 1968, the government inaugurated an evaluation process of the entire cinema sector, with a view to liquidating its financially failing divisions. Subsequently, the writer 'Abd al-Hamid Gouda al-Sahhar was appointed as the chairman of the GEIC, announcing immediately his intention of limiting the public sector's operations solely to co-productions and high-budget films.[80] Around the same time, the minister of finance, taking into consideration the recommendations of the evaluation committee, suggested the consolidation of the Cairo Company for Film Production and the Cairo Company for Film Distribution and Exhibition into one entity, in an attempt to centralize the GEIC's administration and reduce its expenses. This suggestion was taken seriously by Okasha, but not without making a fuss about other problems that the state needed to address immediately to help the GEIC overcome particular difficulties, such as, for example, the high taxes imposed on film stock, the shortage of exhibition houses, and the political tension with neighboring countries. On 30 March 1970, Decree 511 was issued, merging all the public-sector film companies into one body—the General Egyptian Institution for the Cinema (GEIC) (Okasha 2000:770–771). Regardless of this continuous reshuffling of the cinema sector, the GEIC's purpose remained unchanged throughout its existence: sustaining the national film industry, either by producing quality films or by providing services to the private sector. By mid 1970, it had become clear that the Egyptian state was willing to continue its financial support for the public sector as a concession to the latter's past and potential cultural achievements.

On 28 September 1970, Gamal 'Abd al-Nasser died of a heart attack, leaving Egypt in a state of shock and in the hands of his vice-president, Anwar al-Sadat. On 15 May 1971, Sadat launched the Corrective Movement, basically targeting the Nasserist legacy, which included the public sector. As a precursor to his open door policy (*al-infitah*), Sadat launched sequential waves of privatization, inevitably affecting the cinema sector (al-Gayyar 2000:31–32; Sharaffudin 2002:42). On 7 November 1971, the GEIC was dissolved, to be replaced with the General Organization for the Cinema, Theater, and Music (*al-Hay'a

---

80 *Rose al-Yusuf* no. 2090, 1 July 1968, 38–39; *Bulletin d'information du Centre interarabe du cinéma et de la télévision* no. 44, 1 August 1968, 9.

al-'amma li-l-sinima wa-l-masrah wa-l-musiqa).[81] By Decree 2827 of 1971, the public sector was ordered to close down its film production operations, focusing instead on providing film services and facilities to the private sector. In so doing, the public-sector film production prematurely expired, paradoxically at the same time as its own films, produced during and after the downsizing period, were garnering critical acclaim and spawning a second Golden Age of Egyptian cinema.

---

81 Presidential Decree no. 2827 for 1971, *al-Garida al-rasmiya al-misriya* 46, 22 November 1971, 690–691; Armbrust 2010:641.

CHAPTER 5

Conclusion

On 23 January 1972 a member of the Egyptian Parliament drew his colleagues' attention to the heavy financial loss incurred by the now dissolved public-sector film production unit, calling upon the authorities to begin immediate investigations.¹ This deputy's brief intervention in a somewhat ordinary parliamentary session turned into a decade-long trial,² with the apparent intention of redeeming debts and convicting the responsible party.³ Nine years later, on 22 December 1981, the Public Prosecution Office (al-Niyaba al-'amma) in Egypt finally reached a verdict on the basis of the following: given the fact that the public film sector came into being to rescue an imperiled industry; given that the cinema sector was conceived in times of political turbulence; and given that supreme state authorities directed film production to serve the revolutionary regime and its status abroad, the employees of the public sector were deemed not guilty of negligence, as they were operating under extraordinary and extremely difficult circumstances, and in line with general state policy.⁴

This verdict of innocence is absent in much of the existing literature. Even those who refer to it just harp about the problems that the public

---

1   "al-Nas al-kamil li taqrir al-niyaba," 78.
2   Having its own juridical personality made the public sector susceptible to lawsuits. See chapter 3.
3   "al-Nas al-kamil li taqrir al-niyaba," 78.
4   For a complete copy of the court's justification for the verdict, see "al-Nas al-kamil li taqrir al-niyaba," 78–91.

sector faced, which they deemed a complete failure. Although these problems have been discussed at length, this study seeks to emphasize the resolve of the state and its public sector to accomplish its mission of reviving an ailing film industry, in spite of its inherited or acquired problems. Overcoming these difficulties was the first achievement of this sector. The financial and technical support provided by the public film sector to film professionals, working in both the public and private sectors, ensured the continuance of the Egyptian film industry.

The second achievement of the public sector in Egyptian cinema was setting the scene for a new generation of skilled and talented filmmakers. Within an eight-year period, the public sector commissioned 60 directors, who in turn produced 158 films, amounting to almost 30 percent of all Egyptian film production between 1963 and 1971. Among these directors were 26 new names (Abu Shadi 2000b:322–323), some of whom were graduates of the Higher Institute for the Cinema, itself another achievement that is still in operation. Although the public sector ceased its film production in 1971, it still exists as a service sector, under the purview of the General Organization for the Cultural Palaces (al-Hay'a al-'amma li qusur al-thaqafa). The objectives of the current organization are similar to those of its predecessors: publishing specialized books and journals dealing with the cinema; holding film festivals and film weeks; supervising cinema clubs and societies; and encouraging the production of documentary and educational films.

The fourth accomplishment of the public film sector, but one of greater importance, was paving the way for the rise of an alternative cinema, owing to the nourishing environment that this sector helped to create, either through the establishment of the Higher Institute, exposure to international cinematic movements, or its decade-long endeavors to reform the film industry. Even more, the operation of the public sector perpetuated a still existing dilemma of whether films could or should be used for ideological persuasion. The emergence of a new cinematic perception that recognized cinema as a tool for cultural resistance and artistic expression, on a non-profit basis, attests to the public sector's positive influence. The rise of a non-commercial genre in Egyptian filmmaking would assuredly have been more difficult, if not impossible, without the sustenance that the public sector provided.

Conclusion

Now that a more balanced understanding of the public sector has been presented, we may arrive at a better appreciation and assessment of its overall role. A critical analysis of the artistic and creative aspects of the films produced by the public sector now seems possible, without being influenced, not to say tainted, by the preconceived notions that this research seeks to contest.

Besides an analysis dedicated to a thorough examination of film aesthetics and languages, another fruitful research topic would be the under-examined, and perhaps unintended, roles of these films. Instead of dismissing them as artistically insignificant, films produced by the public sector can be analyzed as products of Egyptian history. Though works of fiction, they can still be regarded as cultural artifacts that communicate ideas, stories, perceptions, and dilemmas that prevailed in a specific time period. Not only do they visually represent the sociopolitical, economic, and cultural realities of Nasser's Egypt, but, more importantly, they reflect the visions of their makers—how they perceived the Nasserist experiment as both artists and citizens. One question might be whether these films could be considered a medium for understanding the past—in other words, could they be viewed as a vehicle for legitimate historical analysis?

Another possible investigation is a comparative study between the public sector in Egyptian cinema and its counterparts in other countries such as Algeria, Syria, the Soviet Union, Yugoslavia, Hungary, and China, which were actively increasing the role of public film production in popular mobilization against colonial rule and, following independence, achieving more just and equitable social and political circumstances. This analysis would examine the similarities and differences between these sectors, perhaps with a view to comprehending more fully the particularities of the Egyptian public film sector in terms of theoretical justifications, modes of operation, historical context, and cultural and artistic production. Only then will the pioneering role of the public sector in Egyptian cinema be clearly understood.

Appendix

A List of Films Produced by the Public Sector in Egyptian Cinema
Sources: Abu Shadi 2000a:91–98; Mahmud 2002.

	Film	Director	Release Date
1	Wa-islamah	Andrew Marton	1961
2	al-Nasir Salah al-Din	Youssef Chahine	1963
3	Hadatha fi Misr		1963
4	al-Qahira fi-l-layl	Muhammad Salim	1963
5	Muntaha al-farah	Muhammad Salim	1963
6	al-Aydi al-na'ima	Mahmud Dhulfiqar	1963
7	Bayna al-qasrayn	Hasan al-Imam	1964
8	Zawg fi igaza	Muhammad 'Abd al-Gawad	1964
9	al-Murahiqan	Sayf al-Din Shawkat	1964
10	Harib min al-zawag	Hasan al-Sayfi	1964
11	Min agl hanafi	Hasan al-Sayfi	1964
12	Thaman al-hurriya	Nur al-Damardash	1964
13	I'tirafat zawg	Fatin 'Abd al-Wahab	1964
14	al-Ibn al-mafqud	Muhammad Kamil Hasan	1964
15	Nahr al-hayat	Hasan Rida	1964
16	al-'A'ila al-karima	Fatin 'Abd al-Wahab	1964

Appendix

	Film	Director	Release Date
17	al-Tariq	Husam al-Din Mustafa	1964
18	al-Risala al-akhira	Muhammad Kamil Hasan	1964
19	al-Ragul al-maghul	Muhammad 'Abd al-Gawad	1965
20	al-'Alamayn	Abd al-'Alim Khatab	1965
21	Hiya wa-l-rigal	Hasan al-Imam	1965
22	al-'Aql wa-l-mal	Abbas Kamil	1965
23	al-Haram	Henri Barakat	1965
24	al-Gabal	Khalil Shawqi	1965
25	Tarid al-firdaws	Fatin 'Abd al-Wahab	1965
26	Ayam da'i'a	Baha' al-Din Sharaf	1965
27	Hub li-l-gami'	'Abd al-Rahman Sharif	1965
28	al-Rigal la yatazawagun al-gamilat	Ahmad Faruq	1965
29	Armala wa thalath banat	Galal al-Sharqawi	1965
30	al-Gaza'	'Abd al-Rahman al-Khamisi	1965
31	Sukun al-'asifa	Ahmad Diya' al-Din	1965
32	al-Mustahil	Husayn Kamal	1965
33	al-I'tiraf	Sa'd 'Arafa	1965
34	al-'Inab al-murr	Faruq 'Agrama	1965
35	Aghla min hayati	Mahmud Dhulfiqar	1965
36	al-Thalatha yuhibunaha	Mahmud Dhulfiqar	1965
37	al-Kha'ina	Kamal al-Shaykh	1965
38	Harib min al-ayyam	Husam al-Din Mustafa	1965
39	al-Mamalik	Atif Salim	1965
40	Ibn Kliyubatra		1965
41	Thalathat lusus	Fatin 'Abd al-Wahab, Kamal al-Shaykh, Hasan al-Imam	1965
42	Merati mudir 'amm	Fatin 'Abd al-Wahab	1966
43	Thawrat al-yaman	Atif Salim	1966
44	Wada'an ayuha al-layl	Hasan Rida	1966
45	Sayyid Darwish	Ahmad Badrakhan	1966

Appendix

	Film	Director	Release Date
46	al-Hayah hilwa	Hilmi Halim	1966
47	Saghira 'ala al-hub	Niyazi Mustafa	1966
48	Shayyatin al-layl	Niyazi Mustafa	1966
49	'Adu al-mar'a	Mahmud Dhulfiqar	1966
50	al-Murahiqa al-saghira	Mahmud Dhulfiqar	1966
51	Laylat al-zifaf	Henri Barakat	1966
52	al-Qahira 30	Salah Abu Sayf	1966
53	Khan al-Khalili	Atif Salim	1966
54	Faris bani hamdan	Niyazi Mustafa	1966
55	Kunuz	Hilmi Rafla	1966
56	Shay' fi hayati	Henri Barakat	1966
57	Zawga min Bariz	Atif Salim	1966
58	Ibtisamat Abu al-Haul		1966
59	Qahir al-Atlantis		1966
60	Faris al-sahara'		1966
61	Akhtar ragul fi-l-'alam	Niyazi Mustafa	1967
62	al-Samman wa-l-kharif	Husam al-Din Mustafa	1967
63	Mu'askar al-banat	Khalil Shawqi	1967
64	al-Dakhil	Nur al-Damardash	1967
65	Idrab al-shahatin	Hasan al-Imam	1967
66	al-Layali al-tawila	Mahmud Dhulfiqar	1967
67	al-Qubla al-akhira	Mahmud Dhulfiqar	1967
68	Ma'budat al-gamahir	Hilmi Rafla	1967
69	al-Khurug min al-ganna	Mahmud Dhulfiqar	1967
70	al-Mukharibun	Kamal al-Shaykh	1967
71	'Indama Nuhib	Fatin 'Abd al-Wahab	1967
72	Igazat sayf	Sa'd 'Arafa	1967
73	Gaffat al-amtar	Sayyid 'Issa	1967
74	Garima fi-l-hay al-hadi'	Husam al-Din Mustafa	1967
75	al-Nisf al-akhar	Ahmad Badrakhan	1967

	Film	Director	Release Date
76	al-Zawga al-thaniya	Salah Abu Sayf	1967
77	Gharam fi-l-Karnak	Ali Rida	1967
78	al-'Ayb	Galal al-Sharqawi	1967
79	Nura	Mahmud Dhulfiqar	1967
80	Qasr al-Shawq	Hasan al-Imam	1967
81	Afrah	Ahmad Badrakhan	1968
82	3 Qisas	Ibrahim al-Sahin	1968
83	Ayam al-hub	Hasan Rida, Muhammad Nabih, Hilmi Halim	1968
84	Hawwa' 'ala al-tariq	Husayn Hilmi al-Muhandis	1968
85	Merati magnuna	Hilmi Halim	1968
86	al-Bustagi	Husayn Kamal	1968
87	al-Mutamaridun	Tawfiq Salih	1968
88	al-Qadiya 68	Salah Abu Sayf	1968
89	Gazirat al-'ushaq	Hasan Rida	1968
90	Ard al-nifaq	Fatin 'Abd al-Wahab	1968
91	al-Ragul al-ladhi faqada zilahu	Kamal al-Shaykh	1968
92	Qindil Um Hashim	Kamal 'Atiya	1968
93	Ana al-duktur	Abbas Kamil	1968
94	al-Sirk	Atif Salim	1968
95	Kayfa tasriq milyunaran?	Nagdi Hafiz	1968
96	Kayfa tasriq qunbula dhariya?		1968
97	Abu al-Haul al-Zugagi		1968
98	Shay' min al-khawf	Husayn Kamal	1969
99	Hikaya min baladna	Hilmi Halim	1969
100	Yawmiyat na'ib fi-l-aryaf	Tawfiq Salih	1969
101	al-Nas ili guwa	Galal al-Sharqawi	1969
102	Lusus lakin zurafa'	Ibrahim Lutfi	1969
103	Abwab al-layl	Hasan Rida	1969

Appendix

	Film	Director	Release Date
104	al-Sayyid al-bulti	Tawfiq Salih	1969
105	al-Hilwa 'Aziza	Hasan al-Imam	1969
106	Zawga ghayyura giddan	Hilmi Rafla	1969
107	Akadhib hawwa'	Fatin 'Abd al-Wahab	1969
108	Miramar	Kamal al-Shaykh	1969
109	Wuguh li-l hub	Midhat Bakir, Nagi Riyad, Mamduh Shukri	1969
110	Nadya	Ahmad Badrakhan	1970
111	As'ab zawag	Muhammad Nabih	1970
112	al-Ard	Youssef Chahine	1970
113	Ashya' la tushtara	Ahmad Diya' al-Din	1970
114	Ghurub wa shuruq	Kamal al-Shaykh	1970
115	Harami al-waraqa	Ali Rida	1970
116	Ana wa zawgati wa-l-sikritira	Mahmud Dhulfiqar	1970
117	Awham al-hub	Mamduh Shukri	1970
118	Suq al-harim	Yusuf Marzuq	1970
119	Dalal al-misriya	Hasan al-Imam	1970
120	Nar al-shawq	Muhammad Salim	1970
121	al-Sarrab	Anwar al-Shinnawi	1970
122	Fagr al-Islam	Salah Abu Sayf	1971
123	Malikat al-layl	Hasan Ramzi	1971
124	al-Ikhtiyar	Youssef Chahine	1971
125	Maw'ad ma' al-habib	Hilmi Rafla	1971
126	I'tirafat zawg	Sa'd 'Arafa	1971
127	Mudhakirat al-'anisa manal	Abbas Kamil	1971
128	al-Ba'd ya'ish maratayn	Kamal 'Atiya	1971
129	Rihla ladhidha	Fatin 'Abd al-Wahab	1971
130	Lu'bat kul yawm	Khalil Shawqi	1971
131	Hadithat sharaf	Shafiq Shamiya	1971

	Film	Director	Release Date
132	Zawgati wa-l-kalb	Sa'id Marzuq	1971
133	Nahnu al-rigal tayyibun	Ibrahim Lutfi	1971
134	al-Adwa'	Husayn Hilmi	1972
135	al-Nas wa-l-Nil	Youssef Chahine	1972
136	Bint Badi'a	Hasan al-Imam	1972
137	Ughniya 'ala al-mamar	Ali 'Abd al-Khaliq	1972
138	Suwar mamnu'a	Muhammad 'Abd al-'Aziz, Ashraf Fahmi, Madkur Thabit	1972
139	Laylat hub akhira	Hilmi Rafla	1972
140	al-Hagiz	Muhammad Radi	1972
141	Bayt min rimal	Sa'd 'Arafa	1972
142	al-Shayma'	Husam al-Din Mustafa	1972
143	Hikayat bint ismaha marmar	Henri Barakat	1972
144	Waqr al-ashrar	Hasan al-Sayfi	1972
145	Adwa' al-madina	Fatin 'Abd al-Wahab	1972
146	Layl wa-qudban	Ashraf Fahmi	1972
147	Da'wa li-l-hayah	Midhat Bakir	1972
148	al-Shahat	Husam al-Din Mustafa	1972
149	Zaman ya hub	Atif Salim	1973
150	Zuhur barriya	Yusuf Fransis	1973
151	al-Sullum al-khalfi	Atif Salim	1973
152	al-Ragul al-akhar	Muhammad Basyuni	1973
153	al-Shawari' al-khalfiya	Kamal 'Atiya	1974
154	Armala fi laylat al-zifaf	al-Sayyid Badir	1974
155	al-Mummya'	Shadi 'Abd al-Salam	1975
156	Zilal fi-l-ganib al-'akhar	Ghalib Sha'th	1975
157	al-Talaqi	Subhi Shafiq	1977
158	Gunun al-shabab	Galal al-Sharqawi	1980

References

Primary Sources
Official Documents and Publications
Arab Cinema and Culture: Round Table Conferences under the Auspices and with the Participation of the UNESCO. 1962–1964. 3 vols. Beirut: Arab Film and Television Center.
Arba' mu'tamarat [Four Conferences]. 1967. Cairo: Dar al-Kitab.
Al-Garida al-rasmiya al-misriya [The Official Egyptian Gazette].
"Al-Nas al-kamil li taqrir al-niyaba al-'amma bi hafz al-tahqiq fi qadiyat khasa'ir al-qita' al-'amm al-sinima'i fi Misr" [The Full Text of the Public Prosecution Office's Report Concerning the Financial Loss of the Public Sector in Egyptian Cinema]. 1993. *Al-Sinima wa-l-tarikh* 7: 79–91.
"Qita' al-'amm al-sinima'i fi Misr: taqrir Tharwat 'Ukasha ila ra'is Maglis al-sha'b fi 15 Abril 1972" [The Public Sector in Egyptian Cinema: Tharwat Okasha's Report to the Speaker of the Parliament on 15 April 1972]. 1993. *al-Sinima wa-l-tarikh* 8: 1–45.
Al-Waqa'i' al-misriya [The Egyptian Gazette].

Newspapers and Periodicals
Al-Ahram
Bulletin d'information du Centre interarabe du cinéma et de la télévision
Al-Hilal
Al-Kawakib
Rose al-Yusuf

Al-Tali'a
Al-Thaqafa

Secondary Sources

Abdel-Malek, Anouar. 1968. *Egypt: Military Society, the Army Regime, the Left and Social Change under Nasser.* Translated by Charles Lam Markmann. New York: Random House.

'Abd al-'Aziz, al-Faruq. 1975. "Al-sinima al-misriya wa thawrat yulyu." *al-Tali'a* 11: 139–150.

'Abd al-Wahab, Munir. 1966. "The Cinema and Government." In George Sadoul, ed. *The Cinema in the Arab Countries*, 168–170. Beirut: Interarab Centre of Cinema and Television.

Abu Lughod, Lila. 2005. *Dramas of Nationhood: The Politics of Television in Egypt.* Chicago: University of Chicago Press.

Abu Shadi, 'Ali. 1995. "Chronologie." In Magda Wassef, *Egypte 100 ans de cinéma*, 18–39. Paris: Plume.

———. 2000a. *Al-sinima wa-l-siyasa* [Cinema and Politics]. Cairo: al-Hay'a al-Misriya al-'Amma li-l-Kitab.

———. 2000b. "Al-qita' al-'amm al-sinima'i fi Misr (1963–1972), muhawala li-qira'a mawdu'iya." In *Al-sinima wa-l-siyasa* [Cinema and Politics], 306–325. Cairo: al-Hay'a al-Misriya al-'Amma li-l-Kitab.

———. 2004. *Al-waqa'i' al-sinima al-misriya, 1895–2002* [Chronicles of Egyptian Cinema, 1895–2002]. Cairo: al-Hay'a al-Misriya al-'Amma li-l-Kitab.

Alexander, Anne. 2005. *Nasser.* London: Haus Publishing.

'Ali, Mahmud. 2008. *Ma'at 'amm min al-raqaba 'ala al-sinima al-misriya* [One Hundred Years of Film Censorship in Egypt]. Cairo: al-Maglis al-'Ala li-l-Thaqafa.

Amin, Hussein. 2002. "Freedom as a Value in Arab Media: Perceptions and Attitudes among Journalists," *Political Communications*, 19(2): 125–135.

Armbrust, Walter. 1995. "New Cinema, Commercial Cinema, and the Modernist Tradition in Egypt," *Alif: Journal of Comparative Poetics*, 15, "Arab Cinematics: Toward the New and the Alternative": 81–129.

———. 1996. *Mass Culture and Modernism in Egypt.* Cambridge: Cambridge University Press.

———. 2010. "Cinema and Television in the Arab World." In Robert W. Hefner, ed. *The New Cambridge History of Islam, Muslims and Modernity: Culture and Society since 1800*, 625–647. Cambridge: Cambridge University Press.
al-'Ashari, Muhammad. 1968. "Iqtisadiyat sina'at al-sinima fi Misr: dirasa muqarana" [The Economics of the Film Industry in Egypt: A Comparative Study]. Unpublished PhD diss.: Cairo University.
Ayad, Christophe. 1995. "Le star-système: de la splendeur au voile." In Magda Wassef, ed. *Egypte 100 ans de cinéma*, 134-141. Paris: Plume.
Bahgat, Ahmad Ra'fat, ed. 1996. *Misr mi'at sana sinima* [Egypt: One Hundred Years of Cinema]. Cairo: Matbu'at Mahragan al-Qahira al-Sinima'i al-Dawli al-'Ishrun.
Baker, Raymond. 1974. "Egypt in Shadows, Films and Political Order," *American Behavioral Scientist*, 17(3): 393–423.
Boyd, Douglas A. 1977. "Egyptian Radio: Tool of Political and National Development," *Journalism Monographs*, 48: 3–36.
———. 1982. *Broadcasting in the Arab World: A Survey of Radio and Television in the Middle East*. Philadelphia: Temple University Press.
Crabbs, Jack, Jr. 1975. "Politics, History, and Culture in Nasser's Egypt," *International Journal of Middle East Studies*, 6(4): 386–420.
Crofts, Stephen. 1993. "Reconceptualizing National Cinema/s," *Quarterly Review of Film and Video*, 14(3): 49–67.
Dajani, Karen Finlon. 1980. "Cairo: The Hollywood of the Arab World," *Gazette*, 26: 89–98.
Demiray, Başak Göksel. 2014. "Authorship in Cinema: Author and Reader," *CINEJ Cinema Journal*, 4(1): 5–19.
Diong, Natalie Jia Ning. 2015. "Sawt al-arab or Sawt al-Nasser? The Case of Mass Media under Gamal Abdel Nasser and the Convoluted Rise of Pan-Arabism," *Journal of Georgetown University–Qatar Middle Eastern Studies Student Association*, 1–7.
Farid, Samir. 1973. "al-Qita' al-'amm fi-l-sinima al-misriya," *al-Ma'rifa*, 131: 147-158.
———. 1995. "La censure mode d'emploi." In Magda Wassef, ed. *Egypte 100 ans de cinéma*, 102–116. Paris: Plume.
———. 1999. *Tarikh naqabat al-fannanin fi Misr, 1987–1997* [History of the Artists' Syndicate in Egypt, 1987–1997]. Cairo: al-Hay'a al-Misriya al-'Amma li-l-Kitab.

———. 2001a. *Madkhal ila tarikh al-sinima al-arabiya* [Introduction to the History of Arab Cinema]. Cairo: al-Hay'a al-Misriya al-'Amma li-l-Kitab.

———. 2001b. *Tarikh al-raqaba 'ala al-sinima fi Misr* [History of Film Censorship in Egypt]. Cairo: al-Maktab al-Misri li-Tawzi' al-Matbu'at.

Farugia, Marisa. 2002. "The Plight of Women in Egyptian Cinema, 1940s–1960s." Unpublished PhD diss.: University of Leeds.

Flibbert, Andrew J. 2005. "State and Cinema in Pre-Revolutionary Egypt, 1927–1952." In Arthur Goldschmidt et al., eds. *Re-Envisioning Egypt 1919–1952*, 448–465. Cairo: American University in Cairo Press.

———. 2007. *Commerce in Culture: States and Markets in the World Film Trade*. New York: Palgrave Macmillan.

Franken, Marjorie A. 1996. "Egyptian Cinema and Television: Dancing and the Female Image," *Visual Anthropology*, 8(2–4): 267–285.

Gaffney, Jane. 1987. "The Egyptian Cinema: Industry and Art in a Changing Society," *Arab Studies Quarterly*, 9(1): 53–75.

al-Gamal, Amal. 2008. *al-Sinima al-'arabiya al-mushtaraka, filmughrafya* [Arab Film Co-Production: A Filmography]. Cairo: al-Maglis al-a'la li-l-Thaqafa.

———. 2009. *Aflam al-intag al-mushtarak fi-l-sinima al-misriya, 1946–2006* [Egyptian Film Co-Productions, 1946–2006]. Cairo: al-Hay'a al-'Amma li-Qusur al-Thaqafa.

al-Gayyar, Salwa 'Ali Ibrahim. 2000. *al-Sinima wa-l-siyasa, nash'at al-film al-siyasi wa mu'alagatihi li aham al-qadaya al-siyasiya* [Cinema and Politics: The Origins of the Political Film and Its Treatment of the Most Important Political Problems]. Cairo: al-Maktab al-'Arabi li-l-Ma'arif.

Gordon, Joel. 2001. "Class-Crossed Lovers: Popular Film and Social Change in Nasser's New Egypt," *Quarterly Review of Film and Video*, 18(4): 385–396.

———. 2002. *Revolutionary Melodrama: Popular Film and Civic Identity in Nasser's Egypt*. Chicago: Middle East Documentation Center.

Gürata, Ahmet. 2004. "Tears of Love: Egyptian Cinema in Turkey (1938–1950)," *New Perspectives on Turkey*, 30: 55–82.

Hasan, Ilhami. 1995. *Tarikh al-sinima al-misriya 1896–1970* [History of Egyptian Cinema, 1896–1970]. Cairo: Sanduq al-Tanmiya al-Thaqafiya.
Hatina, Meir. 2004. "History, Politics, and Collective Memory: The Nasserist Legacy in Mubarak's Egypt." In Elie Podeh and Onn Winckler, eds. *Rethinking Nasserism: Revolution and Historical Memory in Modern Egypt*, 100–125. Gainesville: University Press of Florida.
Horton, Alan W. 1962. "A Charter for National Action of the U.A.R," *Northeast Africa Series*, 9(5): 1–20.
Hussein, Taha. 1947. "Jean Paul Sartre wa-l-sinima," *al-Katib al-misri*, 3, 7(26): 179–202.
Johnson, Peter. 1972. "Egypt under Nasser," *MERIP Reports*, 10: 3–12.
Kelsen, Hans. 1964. *The Law of the United Nations: A Critical Analysis of Its Fundamental Problems*. London: Stevens and Sons.
Krishen, Pradip. 1991. "Knocking at the Doors of Public Culture: India's Parallel," *Public Culture*, 4(1): 25–41.
Mahfouz, Medhat. 1995. "Les salles de projection dans l'industrie cinématographique." In Magda Wassef, ed. *Egypte 100 ans de cinéma*, 124-133. Paris: Plume.
Mahmud, Qasim, ed. 2002. *Dalil al-aflam fi-l-qarn al-'ishrin: fi Misr wa-l-'lam al-'arabi*. Cairo: Maktabat Madbuli.
Malkmus, Lizbeth. 1988. "The 'New' Egyptian Cinema, Adapting Genre Conventions to a Changing Society," *Cineaste*, 16(3): 30–33.
Malkmus, Lizbeth, and Roy Armes. 1991. *Arab and African Filmmaking*. London: Zed Books.
Mowlana, Hamid. 1977. "Trends in Middle Eastern Societies." In George Gerbner, ed. *Mass Media Policies in Changing Cultures*, 73–82. New York: John Wiley and Sons.
Mumtaz, I'tidal. 1985. *Mudhakirat raqibat sinima, 30 'aman* [Memoirs of a Film Censor, 30 Years]. Cairo: al-Hay'a al-'Amma li-l-Kitab.
Murad, Sa'id. 1991. "Hiwar ma' Tawfiq Salih" [A Conversation with Tawfiq Salih]. In Sa'id Murad, ed. *Maqalat fi-l-sinima al-'arabiya* [Articles in Arab Cinema], n.p. Beirut: Dar al-Fikr al-Jadid.
Mursi, Ahmad Kamil, and Magdi Wahba. 1973. *Mu'gam al-fann al-sinima'i* [Dictionary of Cinematic Art]. Cairo: al-Hay'a al Misriya al-'Amma li-l-Kitab.

al-Nahas, Hisham. 1994. "Qira'a fi taqrir al-niyaba al-'amma 'an qita' al-'amm al-sinima'i fi Misr [A Reading of the Public Prosecution Office's Report Regarding the Public Film Sector in Egypt]," *al-Sinima wa-l-tarikh*, 10: 21–32.

———, ed. 2010. *al-Sinima al-misriya, al-thawra wa-l-qita' al-'amm 1952–1971, magmu'at abhath* [Egyptian Cinema, the Revolution and the Public Sector, 1952–1971: A Collection of Papers]. Cairo: al-Maglis al-A'la li-l-Thaqafa.

Nash'at, Badr, and Fathi Zaki. 1957. *Muhakamat al-film al-misri: 'ard wa naqd al-sinima al-misriya mundhu nash'atiha* [Egyptian Film on Trial: A Review and Critique of the Egyptian Cinema since Its Inception]. Cairo: Imprimerie La Patrie.

Nasser, Gamal 'Abd al-. 1955. *Egypt's Liberation: The Philosophy of the Revolution*. Translated by Dorothy Thompson. Washington: Public Affairs Press.

Okasha, Tharwat. 2000. *Mudhakirati fi-l-siyasa wa-l-thaqafa* [Memoirs in Politics and Culture]. Cairo: Dar al-Shuruq.

Poudeh, Reza J., and M. Reza Shirvani. 2008. "Issues and Paradoxes in the Development of Iranian National Cinema: An Overview," *Iranian Studies*, 41(3): 323–341.

Qalyubi, Muhammad Kamil. 1980. "al-Sinima al-misriya, da'irat al-hisar wa rihlat al-khurug," *al-Thaqafa al-Gadida*, 15: 61–71.

———. 1995. "L'enseignement du cinéma." In Magda Wassef, ed. *Egypte 100 ans de cinéma*, 94–101. Paris: Plume.

Sadoul, George, ed. 1966. *The Cinema in the Arab Countries*. Beirut: Interarab Centre of Cinema and Television.

Sa'id, Sayyid. 1994. "Waqfa ... wa nazra li-l-takhaluf qabla an nakhyu li-l-amam." In Madkur Thabit, ed. *Awraq fi mushkilat i'adat al-ta'rikh li-l-sinima al-misriya* [Problems in the Historiography of Egyptian Cinema], 1–37. Cairo: Akadimiyat al-Funun.

Samak, Qussai. 1977. "The Politics of Egyptian Cinema," *MERIP Reports*, 56: 12–15.

———. 1979. "The Arab Cinema and the National Question, from the Trivial to the Sacrosanct," *Cineaste* 9(3): 32–34.

Shafik, Viola. 2007a. *Arab Cinema: History and Cultural Identity*. Cairo: American University in Cairo Press.

――――. 2007b. *Popular Egyptian Cinema: Gender, Class, and Nation.* Cairo: American University in Cairo Press.
Sharaffudin, Durriya. 2002. *al-Siyasa wa-l-sinima fi Misr, 1961–1981* [Politics and Cinema in Egypt, 1971–1981]. Cairo: al-Hay'a al-Misriya al-'Amma li-l-Kitab.
al-Sharqawi, Galal. 1966a. "History of the U.A.R. Cinema 1896–1962." In George Sadoul, ed. *The Cinema in the Arab Countries*, 69-97. Beirut: Interarab Centre of Cinema and Television.
――――. 1966b. "Languages in the Arab Countries." In George Sadoul, ed. *The Cinema in the Arab Countries*, 61–68. Beirut: Interarab Centre of Cinema and Television.
――――. 1970. *Risala fi tarikh al-sinima al-arabiya* [A Thesis on the History of Arab Cinema]. Cairo: al-Hay'a al-Misriya al-'Amma li-l-Kitab.
Shohat, Ella. 1983. "Egypt: Cinema and Revolution," *Critical Arts*, 2(4): 22–32.
Solanas, Fernando, and Octavio Getino. 1997. "Towards a Third Cinema: Notes and Experiences for the Development of a Cinema of Liberation in the Third World." In Michael T. Martin, ed. *New Latin America Cinema: Theory, Practices and Transcontinental Articulations*, vol. 1, 33–58. Detroit: Wayne State University Press.
Stam, Robert. 2000. *Film Theory: An Introduction.* Oxford: Blackwell.
Stephens, Robert. 1971. *Nasser: A Political Biography.* London: Allen Lane/Penguin Press.
Tawfiq, Sa'd al-Din. N.d. *Qisat al-sinima fi Misr, dirasa naqdiya* [The Story of the Cinema in Egypt: A Critical Study]. Egypt: Dar al-Hilal.
Thabit, Madkur. 1994. "Hawla nash'at wa tatawur sina'at al-sinima fi Misr wa waqi'iha." In Madkur Thabet, ed. *Awraq fi mushkilat i'adat al-ta'rikh li-l-sinima al-misriya* [Problems in the Historiography of Egyptian Cinema], 1–37. Cairo: Akadimiyat al-Funun.
Thoraval, Yves. 2000. *Regard sur le cinéma égyptien.* Paris: Edition L'Harmattan.
Tignor, Robert L. 1998. *Capitalism and Nationalism at the End of Empire: State and Business in Decolonizing Egypt, Nigeria, and Kenya, 1945–1963.* Princeton: Princeton University Press.
al-Tilimsani, May. 1994 (trans.). *al-Sinima al-arabiya min al-khalig ila al-muhit* [Arab Cinema from the Gulf to the Ocean]. Cairo: al-Hay'a al-Misriya al-'Amma li-l-Kitab.

———. 1995. "Sinima al-dawla sinima badila, qira'a fi tagrubat al-qita' al-'amm al sinima'i fi Misr" [National Cinema as an Alternative Cinema in Egypt], *Alif: Journal of Comparative Poetics*, 15, "Arab Cinematics: Toward the New and the Alternative": 70–84.

Wahba, Magdi. 1972. *Cultural Policy in Egypt*. Paris: UNESCO.

Wassef, Magda, ed. 1995. *Egypte 100 ans de cinéma*. Paris: Plume.

Waterbury, John. 1983. *The Egypt of Nasser and Sadat: The Political Economy of Two Regimes*. Princeton: Princeton University Press.

About the Author

Tamara C. Maatouk is is a history Ph.D. student at the Graduate Center, City University of New York, with a focus on the modern Middle East. This monograph is based on her MA thesis in history, the American University of Beirut.

CAIRO PAPERS IN SOCIAL SCIENCE

Volume One
1   *Women, Health and Development*, Cynthia Nelson, ed.
2   *Democracy in Egypt*, Ali E. Hillal Dessouki, ed.
3   *Mass Communications and the October War*, Olfat Hassan Agha
4   *Rural Resettlement in Egypt*, Helmy Tadros
5   *Saudi Arabian Bedouin*, Saad E. Ibrahim and Donald P. Cole

Volume Two
1   *Coping with Poverty in a Cairo Community*, Andrea B. Rugh
2   *Modernization of Labor in the Arab Gulf*, Enid Hill
3   *Studies in Egyptian Political Economy*, Herbert M. Thompson
4   *Law and Social Change in Contemporary Egypt*, Cynthia Nelson and Klaus Friedrich Koch, eds.
5   *The Brain Drain in Egypt*, Saneya Saleh

Volume Three
1   *Party and Peasant in Syria*, Raymond Hinnebusch
2   *Child Development in Egypt*, Nicholas V. Ciaccio
3   *Living without Water*, Asaad Nadim et al.
4   *Export of Egyptian School Teachers*, Suzanne A. Messiha
5   *Population and Urbanization in Morocco*, Saad E. Ibrahim

Volume Four
1   *Cairo's Nubian Families*, Peter Geiser
2, 3 *Symposium on Social Research for Development: Proceedings*, Social Research Center
4   *Women and Work in the Arab World*, Earl L. Sullivan and Karima Korayem

Volume Five
1   *Ghagar of Sett Guiranha: A Study of a Gypsy Community in Egypt*, Nabil Sobhi Hanna
2   *Distribution of Disposal Income and the Impact of Eliminating Food Subsidies in Egypt*, Karima Korayem
3   *Income Distribution and Basic Needs in Urban Egypt*, Amr Mohie el-Din

Volume Six
1. *The Political Economy of Revolutionary Iran*, Mihssen Kadhim
2. *Urban Research Strategies in Egypt*, Richard A. Lobban, ed.
3. *Non-alignment in a Changing World*, Mohammed el-Sayed Selim, ed.
4. *The Nationalization of Arabic and Islamic Education in Egypt: Dar al-Alum and al-Azhar*, Lois A. Aroian

Volume Seven
1. *Social Security and the Family in Egypt*, Helmi Tadros
2. *Basic Needs, Inflation and the Poor of Egypt*, Myrette el-Sokkary
3. *The Impact of Development Assistance on Egypt*, Earl L. Sullivan, ed.
4. *Irrigation and Society in Rural Egypt*, Sohair Mehanna, Richard Huntington, and Rachad Antonius

Volume Eight
1, 2 *Analytic Index of Survey Research in Egypt*, Madiha el-Safty, Monte Palmer, and Mark Kennedy

Volume Nine
1. *Philosophy, Ethics and Virtuous Rule*, Charles E. Butterworth
2. *The 'Jihad': An Islamic Alternative in Egypt*, Nemat Guenena
3. *The Institutionalization of Palestinian Identity in Egypt*, Maha A. Dajani
4. *Social Identity and Class in a Cairo Neighborhood*, Nadia A. Taher

Volume Ten
1. *Al-Sanhuri and Islamic Law*, Enid Hill
2. *Gone for Good*, Ralph Sell
3. *The Changing Image of Women in Rural Egypt*, Mona Abaza
4. *Informal Communities in Cairo: the Basis of a Typology*, Linda Oldham, Haguer el Hadidi, and Hussein Tamaa

Volume Eleven
1. *Participation and Community in Egyptian New Lands: The Case of South Tahrir*, Nicholas Hopkins et al.
2. *Palestinian Universities under Occupation*, Antony T. Sullivan
3. *Legislating Infitah: Investment, Foreign Trade and Currency Laws*, Khaled M. Fahmy
4. *Social History of an Agrarian Reform Community in Egypt*, Reem Saad

Volume Twelve
1 *Cairo's Leap Forward: People, Households, and Dwelling Space*, Fredric Shorter
2 *Women, Water, and Sanitation: Household Water Use in Two Egyptian Villages*, Samiha el-Katsha et al.
3 *Palestinian Labor in a Dependent Economy: Women Workers in the West Bank Clothing Industry*, Randa Siniora
4 *The Oil Question in Egyptian-Israeli Relations, 1967–1979: A Study in International Law and Resource Politics*, Karim Wissa

Volume Thirteen
1 *Squatter Markets in Cairo*, Helmi R. Tadros, Mohamed Feteeha, and Allen Hibbard
2 *The Sub-culture of Hashish Users in Egypt: A Descriptive Analytic Study*, Nashaat Hassan Hussein
3 *Social Background and Bureaucratic Behavior in Egypt*, Earl L. Sullivan, el Sayed Yassin, Ali Leila, and Monte Palmer
4 *Privatization: The Egyptian Debate*, Mostafa Kamel el-Sayyid

Volume Fourteen
1 *Perspectives on the Gulf Crisis*, Dan Tschirgi and Bassam Tibi
2 *Experience and Expression: Life among Bedouin Women in South Sinai*, Deborah Wickering
3 *Impact of Temporary International Migration on Rural Egypt*, Atef Hanna Nada
4 *Informal Sector in Egypt*, Nicholas S. Hopkins, ed.

Volume Fifteen
1 *Scenes of Schooling: Inside a Girls' School in Cairo*, Linda Herrera
2 *Urban Refugees: Ethiopians and Eritreans in Cairo*, Dereck Cooper
3 *Investors and Workers in the Western Desert of Egypt: An Exploratory Survey*, Naeim Sherbiny, Donald Cole, and Nadia Makary
4 *Environmental Challenges in Egypt and the World*, Nicholas S. Hopkins, ed.

Volume Sixteen
1 *The Socialist Labor Party: A Case Study of a Contemporary Egyptian Opposition Party*, Hanaa Fikry Singer
2 *The Empowerment of Women: Water and Sanitation Initiatives in Rural Egypt*, Samiha el Katsha and Susan Watts
3 *The Economics and Politics of Structural Adjustment in Egypt: Third Annual Symposium*

4   *Experiments in Community Development in a Zabbaleen Settlement*, Marie Assaad and Nadra Garas

Volume Seventeen
1   *Democratization in Rural Egypt: A Study of the Village Local Popular Council*, Hanan Hamdy Radwan
2   *Farmers and Merchants: Background for Structural Adjustment in Egypt*, Sohair Mehanna, Nicholas S. Hopkins, and Bahgat Abdelmaksoud
3   *Human Rights: Egypt and the Arab World, Fourth Annual Symposium*
4   *Environmental Threats in Egypt: Perceptions and Actions*, Salwa S. Gomaa, ed.

Volume Eighteen
1   *Social Policy in the Arab World*, Jacqueline Ismael and Tareq Y. Ismael
2   *Workers, Trade Union and the State in Egypt: 1984–1989*, Omar el-Shafie
3   *The Development of Social Science in Egypt: Economics, History and Sociology; Fifth Annual Symposium*
4   *Structural Adjustment, Stabilization Policies and the Poor in Egypt*, Karima Korayem

Volume Nineteen
1   *Nilopolitics: A Hydrological Regime, 1870–1990*, Mohamed Hatem el-Atawy
2   *Images of the Other: Europe and the Muslim World before 1700*, David R. Blanks et al.
3   *Grass Roots Participation in the Development of Egypt*, Saad Eddin Ibrahim et al.
4   *The Zabbalin Community of Muqattam*, Elena Volpi and Doaa Abdel Motaal

Volume Twenty
1   *Class, Family, and Power in an Egyptian Village*, Samer el-Karanshawy
2   *The Middle East and Development in a Changing World*, Donald Heisel, ed.
3   *Arab Regional Women's Studies Workshop*, Cynthia Nelson and Soraya Altorki, eds.
4   *"Just a Gaze": Female Clientele of Diet Clinics in Cairo: An Ethnomedical Study*, Iman Farid Bassyouny

Volume Twenty-one
1   *Turkish Foreign Policy during the Gulf War of 1990–1991*, Mostafa Aydin
2   *State and Industrial Capitalism in Egypt*, Samer Soliman
3   *Twenty Years of Development in Egypt (1977–1997): Part I*, Mark C. Kennedy
4   *Twenty Years of Development in Egypt (1977–1997): Part II*, Mark C. Kennedy

Volume Twenty-two
1 *Poverty and Poverty Alleviation Strategies in Egypt*, Ragui Assaad and Malak Rouchdy
2 *Between Field and Text: Emerging Voices in Egyptian Social Science*, Seteney Shami and Linda Hererra, eds.
3 *Masters of the Trade: Crafts and Craftspeople in Cairo, 1750–1850*, Pascale Ghazaleh
4 *Discourses in Contemporary Egypt: Politics and Social Issues*, Enid Hill, ed.

Volume Twenty-three
1 *Fiscal Policy Measures in Egypt: Public Debt and Food Subsidy*, Gouda Abdel-Khalek and Karima Korayem
2 *New Frontiers in the Social History of the Middle East*, Enid Hill, ed.
3 *Egyptian Encounters*, Jason Thompson, ed.
4 *Women's Perception of Environmental Change in Egypt*, Eman el Ramly

Volume Twenty-four
1, 2 *The New Arab Family*, Nicholas S. Hopkins, ed.
3 *An Investigation of the Phenomenon of Polygyny in Rural Egypt*, Laila S. Shahd
4 *The Terms of Empowerment: Islamic Women Activists in Egypt*, Sherine Hafez

Volume Twenty-five
1, 2 *Elections in the Middle East: What Do They Mean?* Iman A. Hamdy, ed.
3 *Employment Crisis of Female Graduates in Egypt: An Ethnographic Account*, Ghada F. Barsoum
4 *Palestinian and Israeli Nationalism: Identity Politics and Education in Jerusalem*, Evan S. Weiss

Volume Twenty-six
1 *Culture and Natural Environment: Ancient and Modern Middle Eastern Texts*, Sharif S. Elmusa, ed.
2 *Street Children in Egypt: Group Dynamics and Subcultural Constituents*, Nashaat Hussein
3 *IMF–Egyptian Debt Negotiations*, Bessma Momani
4 *Forced Migrants and Host Societies in Egypt and Sudan*, Fabienne Le Houérou

Volume Twenty-seven
1, 2 *Cultural Dynamics in Contemporary Egypt*, Maha Abdelrahman, Iman A. Hamdy, Malak Rouchdy, and Reem Saad, eds.

3 *The Role of Local Councils in Empowerment and Poverty Reduction*, Solava Ibrahim
4 *Beach Politics: Gender and Sexuality in Dahab*, Mustafa Abdalla

Volume Twenty-eight
1 *Creating Families across Boundaries: A Case Study of Romanian/Egyptian Mixed Marriages*, Ana Vinea
2, 3 *Pioneering Feminist Anthropology in Egypt: Selected Writings from Cynthia Nelson*, Martina Rieker, ed.
4 *Roses in Salty Soil: Women and Depression in Egypt Today*, Dalia A. Mostafa

Volume Twenty-nine
1 *Crossing Borders, Shifting Boundaries: Palestinian Dilemmas*, Sari Hanafi, ed.
2, 3 *Political and Social Protest in Egypt*, Nicholas S. Hopkins, ed.
4 *The Experience of Protest: Masculinity and Agency among Sudanese Refugees in Cairo*, Martin T. Rowe

Volume Thirty
1 *Child Protection Policies in Egypt: A Rights-Based Approach*, Adel Azer, Sohair Mehanna, Mulki Al-Sharmani, and Essam Ali
2 *"The Farthest Place": Social Boundaries in an Egyptian Desert Community*, Joseph Viscomi
3 *The New York Egyptians: Voyages and Dreams*, Yasmine M. Ahmed
4 *The Burden of Resources: Oil and Water in the Gulf and the Nile Basin*, Sharif S. Elmusa, ed.

Volume Thirty-one
1 *Humanist Perspectives on Sacred Space*, David Blanks, Bradley S. Clough, eds.
2 *Law as a Tool for Empowering Women within Marital Relations: A Case Study of Paternity Lawsuits in Egypt*, Hind Ahmed Zaki
3, 4 *Visual Productions of Knowledge: Toward a Different Middle East*, Hanan Sabea, Mark R. Westmoreland, eds.

Volume Thirty-two
1 *Planning Egypt's New Settlements: The Politics of Spatial Inequities*, Dalia Wahdan
2 *Agrarian Transformation in the Arab World: Persistent and Emerging Challenges*, Habib Ayeb and Reem Saad

3   *Femininity and Dance in Egypt: Embodiment and Meaning in al-Raqs al-Baladi*, Noha Roushdy
4   *Negotiating Space: The Evolution of the Egyptian Street, 2000–2011*, Dimitris Soudias

Volume Thirty-three

1   *Masculinities in Egypt and the Arab World: Historical, Literary, and Social Science Perspectives*, Helen Rizzo, ed.
2   *Anthropology in Egypt 1900–1967: Culture, Function, and Reform*, Nicholas S. Hopkins
3   *The Church in the Square: Negotiations of Religion and Revolution at an Evangelical Church in Cairo*, Anna Jeannine Dowell
4   *The Political Economy of the New Egyptian Republic*, Nicholas S. Hopkins, ed.

Volume Thirty-four

1   *Egyptian Hip-Hop: Expressions from the Underground*, Ellen R. Weis
2   *Sports and Society in the Middle East*, Nicholas S. Hopkins and Sandrine Gamblin, eds.
3   *Organizing the Unorganized: Migrant Domestic Workers in Lebanon*, Farah Kobaissy
4   *The Food Question in the Middle East*, Malak S. Rouchdy and Iman A. Hamdy, eds.

Volume Thirty-five

1   *Oral History in Times of Change: Gender, Documentation, and the Making of Archives*, Hoda Elsadda and Hanan Sabea, eds.
2   *International Migration in the Euro-Mediterranean Region*, Ibrahim Awad, ed.

www.ingramcontent.com/pod-product-compliance
Lightning Source LLC
Chambersburg PA
CBHW071919070526
44583CB00016B/2054